D0910355

MARK TWAIN'S
88 DAYS IN THE MOTHER LODE
& Stories of the Gold Rush

Written and Compiled by James Fletcher

Samuel Clemens at close to 18 years of age, circa 1851
Photo courtesy of the Mark Twain Project—
The Bancroft Library, University of California, Berkeley

Manzanita Writers Press
San Andreas, California

Mark Twain's 88 Days in the Mother Lode
& Stories of the Gold Rush

Copyright © 2015 by Jim Fletcher

ISBN: 978-0-9908019-1-7
Library of Congress Control Number: 2015940453

Cover Credits:

Front Cover: Top right illustration courtesy of the Mark Twain Project—The Bancroft Library, University of California, Berkeley.

Montage clockwise from top left: Gillis Cabin on Jackass Hill courtesy of John Meiser and the Mark Twain Project—The Bancroft Library, University of California, Berkeley; Portrait of Mark Twain, Bicknell Engraving, courtesy of the Mark Twain Project—The Bancroft Library, University of California, Berkeley; Angels Hotel, courtesy of the Calaveras Historical Society; Jim Gillis on the bench, courtesy of Bank of Stockton Archives.

Cover, Book Design and Production: Connie Strawbridge

To order copies directly from the publisher:

Manzanita Writers Press
A member of the Literary League of the Calaveras County Arts Council
PO Box 632, San Andreas, CA 95249
Editor, Monika Rose
mrosemanza@jps.net
www.manzapress.com
(209) 754-0577

All rights reserved. No portion of this book may be reproduced in any form without written permission from the publisher.

Printed in the United States of America.

Town of Melones on the Stanislaus River, prior to building of the dam ~ Jackass Hill is to the south in Tuolumne County, Angels Camp is to the north. Robinson's Ferry was used to cross this river. Photo courtesy of the Calaveras County Historical Society

New Melones Reservoir in a plentiful water year ~
Photo courtesy of Wallace Motlock and the Calaveras County Historical Society

Cabin replica on Jackass Hill as it appears today by James Fletcher

TABLE OF CONTENTS

TABLE OF CONTENTS

INTRODUCTION

In February 2015 a new Mark Twain documentary film debuted. Produced by John C. Brown and Bert Simonis, *88 Days in the Mother Lode: Mark Twain Finds His Voice*, portraying the experiences of Mark Twain during his stay on Jackass Hill in the winter of 1864, premiered in Angels Camp. This book, *Mark Twain's 88 Days in the Mother Lode & Stories of the Gold Rush*, soon followed.

But why a new movie and book? Because of the fascinating, wonderful stories they tell about the life of Sam Clemens, who would become Mark Twain, and the extraordinary people and adventures he would share during his 88-day stay in the Mother Lode, a story I learned about just a few years ago.

Sherri Smith, Owner of Camps Restaurant at Greenhorn Creek Resort, Bob Rogers, then Director of the Angels Camp Museum, and I, a retired history teacher living in the Mother Lode, were discussing the legacy and history of Mark Twain. We all agreed there were few places for a visitor to go, on a regular basis, to hear the story of Mark Twain's journey to the Mother Lode and Jackass Hill, and how that experience may have influenced his life and literary legacy.

Sherri asked me if I knew much about Mark Twain and his time in the Mother Lode, and I said not much, but I'd start investigating.

Where to start? Ken Burns—I admire Ken Burns. He makes the history of our country come alive as we learn so much about the Civil War, jazz, baseball, Lewis & Clark, the West, and Mark Twain. His documentary film, *Mark Twain*, is amazing—it is a memorable history and heart-breaking journey through the triumphs and tragedies of Twain's life.

Another source of inspiration is Pulitzer Prize winner and co-author of *Flags of Our Fathers*, Ron Powers, who wrote *Mark Twain: A Life*, the current and most impressive scholarly work about Mark Twain. This is a massive work of historical research and writing that illuminates the very fabric of Twain's life.

Then, there was Mark Twain's own *Autobiography* written toward the end of his life. The book contains all manner of anecdotes, remembrances, descriptions, and personal observations, including commentaries about Jim Gillis and the Gillis clan. Albert Bigelow Paine wrote and published *Mark Twain, a Biography,* a four-volume work published in 1912, which included retracing Twain's journey into the West and his stay on Jackass Hill.

George Williams III has written an entire series of books about Mark Twain's life and adventures in the West. Three of his books, *Mark Twain: His Adventures in Aurora; Mark Twain: His Life in Virginia City, Nevada;* and *Mark Twain and the Jumping Frog of Calaveras County,* are well researched histories about Twain's times in the West and on Jackass Hill in the winter of 1864-1865, including a history of the frog story.

Billy Gillis, the brother of Steve and Jim Gillis, wrote several volumes about the 88-day period of time when Mark Twain lived with him in a little cabin on Jackass Hill. Billy wrote a personal history, *Goldrush Days with Mark Twain* in 1930, and a second edition, *Memories of Mark Twain and Steve Gillis,* was later published. They are his first-person accounts of life during the Gold Rush and remembrances of his days with Sam Clemens.

Regional resources were immensely helpful in my research. Robert Gordon, a local historian, and the staff at the Tuolumne County Historical Society in Sonora, CA, a dedicated, knowledgeable, friendly group of volunteers, provided access to a tremendous archive filled with all kinds of information about people like the Gillis clan, Mark Twain, and Mother Lode legend and lore. The museum and archives in Sonora is a wonderful place to visit and enjoy discovering Mother Lode history. Another source for invaluable historical research was the Calaveras Historical Society in San Andreas, CA.

The Mark Twain Papers and Project at the Bancroft Library, UC Berkeley, is the home of almost everything Mark Twain. Mr. Robert Hirst, General Editor, and Mr. Victor Fisher, Principal Editor, were engaging, helpful Mark Twain resources who knew virtually everything about his history and provided photos, manuscripts, and all manner of Twain memorabilia. The University of California Press has published a wealth of Twain's personal books, like *Roughing It*, and reference works like *Mark Twain's Notebooks and Journals, Volumes I and II*. Photos, letters, manuscripts, and even "Notebook 4," are carefully preserved for anyone to see and investigate at the Bancroft library.

And, after all the reading, research, and listening, I discovered there was a fascinating story to tell, especially about Sam Clemens' journey west, how he came to Jackass Hill, and the extraordinary men who shared those days with him—Jim Gillis, Dick Stoker, and Billy Gillis.

In the fall of 2013, Sherri turned the small dining area at Camps Restaurant into the Mark Twain Library, and I started presenting a one-hour weekly program, "88 Days in the Mother Lode," describing the Gold Rush and Mark Twain's early life and journey to Jackass Hill.

The program was warmly received by visitors as well as people living in the area. The staff at the Calaveras County Visitors Center in Angels Camp, Mrs. Judy Poseman, Ms. Lisa Boulton, Mrs. Penny Mortimer, and Mrs. Sandy Price, continued to recommend the program to visitors and encouraged us to continue.

I asked John C. Brown, an independent filmmaker living in Sonora, to come to one of the programs. John and his partner, Bert Simonis, produce award-winning films for their company called

This 'n That Films. After seeing the program, John agreed that there was, indeed, a wonderful story to tell about Mark Twain and his 88 days on the hill, which inspired him to begin working on a new film, *88 Days in the Mother Lode: Mark Twain Finds His Voice*.

Greenhorn Creek contributed to the film as well. Mike Kristoff, Manager of Greenhorn Creek Resort, and Sherri Smith, Owner of Camps Restaurant, each contributed $2,500 toward the film project and became co-producers. Bob Kolakowski, a semi-retired, genial, and history-loving keeper of the bar at Greenhorn Creek Resort was one of the four or five people I invited to see the "pilot" of the one-hour program I was preparing in the library and was very supportive of our efforts. Bob was also the first person I asked to read whatever I wrote, and his comments and recommendations were greatly appreciated.

The movie was produced and released, but what about a book? I sought the help of Monika Rose, Director and Editor of Manzanita Writer Press, in San Andreas. Monika works with a regional group of stellar poets and writers who meet on a regular basis to listen to and make recommendations for new works being written by published and not-yet-published writers. I took the very first 20 pages I had written for this book and read it to the group. I had grammar problems and the manuscript needed serious editing—but, they LIKED the 88-Days story! Everyone thought this was a truly important history to tell about the Mother Lode, and they thought that it would make a great book.

Both Monika Rose, Editor/Director, and Connie Strawbridge, Marketing Director, Graphic Designer/Book Designer of Manzanita Writers Press, have worked with me to bring this book to life.

DEDICATION

Two years ago, I didn't know much about Mark Twain or his 88-day stay on Jackass Hill, and now there is a movie and a book about his life and times in the Mother Lode. As stated in the introduction, all the Twain history, biographies, memories, personal commentaries, and other literary sources were written by many, many people before I ever started trying to write and compile the material for this book. For the last two years, everyone connected with the film and book have been incredibly helpful, encouraging, and supportive of our efforts to retell this fascinating story, both in the film and the book.

I would like to dedicate my book to all of those who support projects like the *88 Days* film—and this book, which strives to provide a continuing awareness of the very special history and legacy of Mark Twain, his time in the West, and those important and life-changing 88 days he spent on Jackass Hill in the company of men he admired and respected—Jim Gillis, Dick Stoker, and Billy Gillis.

As the title notes, I did not write this book, I compiled it. Most of the words and descriptions are from the works of historians or authors like Albert Paine, George Williams III, Mark Twain, Billy Gillis, and other sources to help retell this remarkable story. If I have not identified or given proper accreditation to a comment, description, or quotation, that was not my intent.

It is my hope the reader will enjoy the journey as much as I have over these past few years.

Respectfully,

Jim Fletcher
aka Miner Jim

SAM CLEMENS JOURNEYS WEST

" I spent three months in the log-cabin home of Jim Gillis and his 'pard' Dick Stoker, in Jackass Gulch, that serene and reposeful and dreamy and delicious sylvan paradise. "

~ From a letter Mark Twain wrote in remembrance of Jim Gillis in 1907

Like Halley's Comet that announced the beginning and end of his life, Sam Clemens, later known as Mark Twain, would leave a brilliant, wondrous legacy across America and the world. He would become one of the most recognized faces and names on the planet—a man enormously respected and revered for his literature, public lectures, and scathing attacks on corruption, greed, inhumanity, and racial hatred. He was also a man who used humor to mask the heartbreaking tragedies and terrible emotional pain that accompanied him throughout his life.

Mark Twain began his life in poverty, climbed to the greatest heights of financial success, and lost it all in bankruptcy by the age of 60. In Hartford, Connecticut, he built one of the most famous homes in America for his wife and three daughters, a marvelous mansion that was the family's refuge, a stopping place for every celebrity and literary person of note. It was also a home in which his beloved daughter Suzy would die an early and tragic death while the family was in Europe; he visited the home only once more in his life after her death.

Twain's early life would be lived in stages, set pieces where he would experience and remember people, places, and events and incorporate them into his writings. Hannibal was his boyhood home, and *The Adventures of Tom Sawyer* and *The Adventures of Huckleberry Finn* were tales resulting from memories of those days. He lived his early adult life on the Mississippi River as a steamboat pilot, chronicled in *Life on the Mississippi*, and might well have remained there for the rest of his life but for the Civil War.

Escaping the carnage of war, Sam Clemens traveled west with his brother, Orion, to the new Nevada Territory and the riches of the Comstock Lode, adventures he would retell in *Roughing It*. He failed as a miner, timber owner, mill worker, and every other vocation he undertook. On the brink of abject poverty, he was hired by owner Joe Goodman to be the City Editor of the *Territorial Enterprise* and spent the next 19 months learning the craft of writing.

But Sam wore out his welcome in Virginia City, and along with his friend Steve Gillis, moved to San Francisco. At first a successful writer, Twain found that his fortunes would turn for the worse when he lost his savings in mining stocks as well as his job as a reporter. Virtually penniless, with little or no hope for the future, and slinking from backstreet to backstreet, he contemplated suicide.

Then, Steve Gillis would get into a barroom fight, and that led to the marvelous story of Sam Clemens' 88 days in the Mother Lode, one of the most important episodes of his life, and one which would help catapult him to worldwide fame as Mark Twain, both as a writer and performer. To better understand how Sam Clemens became Mark Twain, we must begin where it all started.

Jane Lampton married John Marshall Clemens in 1823. Clemens, 25, according to Twain biographer Paine, was "sober, industrious, and unswervingly upright." Jane, 20, was "gay, buoyant,

Jane Lampton Clemens, photo courtesy of the Mark Twain Project—
The Bancroft Library, University of California, Berkeley

celebrated for her beauty and her grace; able to dance all night, and all day too, for that matter . . . . Many of the characteristics that made Mark Twain famous were inherited from his mother. His sense of humor, his prompt, quaintly spoken philosophy, these were distinctly her contribution to his fame." Twain would later say, "She had a sort of ability which is rare in man and hardly existent in woman—the ability to say a humorous thing with the perfect air of not knowing it to be humorous." Only four of Jane's children would reach adulthood—Orion (1825), Pamela (1827), Sam (1835), and Henry (1838) (Paine, Chapter 2).

In 1835, John Clemens moved his family to the tiny new town of Florida, Missouri, at the urging of a relative of Jane's, John Quarles, to open a general store and begin selling land around Florida to those moving ever west. Samuel Langhorne Clemens, her sixth baby, was born prematurely on November 30, 1835, in Florida. "It was not a robust childhood. The new baby managed to go through the winter—a matter of comment among the family and neighbors. Added strength came, but slowly; 'Little Sam,' as they called him, was always delicate during those early years" (Paine, Chapter 2).

John Quarles, who Twain thought was one of the finest men he had ever known, owned a 500-acre farm near Florida, which included fifteen to twenty slaves to do the work. The Clemens family would visit the farm in the summer, and Sam discovered in the slave's quarters two of the most important influences in his young life, Aunt Hannah and Uncle Dan'l.

Aunt Hannah, Twain noted in his *Autobiography*, "we believed was upward of a thousand years old and had talked with Moses . . . . She had a round bald place on the crown of her head and we used to creep around and gaze at it in reverent silence and reflect that it was caused by fright through seeing Pharaoh drowned. She was also superstitious and had great faith in prayer, prayer she employed whenever witches were around."

Uncle Dan'l was a middle-aged slave, and as Twain described, "a faithful and affectionate good friend, ally and adviser . . . whose sympathies were wide and warm and whose heart was honest and simple and knew no guile. He has served me well these many, many years. I have not seen him for more than half a century and yet spiritually I have had his welcome company a good part of that time and have staged him in books under his own name and as 'Jim,' and carted him all around—to Hannibal, down the Mississippi on a raft and even across the Desert of Sahara in a balloon—and he has endured it all with the patience and friendliness and loyalty which were his birthright" (*Autobiography*, Chapter 2).

MOVING TO HANNIBAL

John Clemens suffered from a continuing series of financial failures that forced the family to move again to Hannibal, Missouri, on the banks of the Mississippi River when Sam was four. Hannibal was every adventurous child's dream come true. It sat on a river that had a busy and bustling life, with entertainments like swimming, rafting, and exploring caves. The boys spent endless days on river islands fishing, smoking cob pipes, and creating all manner of mischief for the adults of the town. Sam had a close friend in Tom Blankenship, the son of a local drunk, and the two of them would spend day and night together. "In Huckleberry Finn I have drawn Tom Blankenship exactly as he was. He was ignorant, unwashed, insufficiently fed; but he had as good a heart as ever any boy had. His liberties were totally unrestricted. He was the only really independent person—boy or man—in the community, and by consequence he was tranquilly and continuously happy and was envied by all the rest of us" (*Autobiography*, Chapter 14).

John Clemens' financial condition continued to worsen, and the family was almost bankrupt. There was hope, however, that their fortunes would be made secure if he was elected to the office of clerkship of the Surrogate Court. He was widely respected for his honesty and integrity, and there was general sympathy for the condition of the Clemens family. He was easily elected, and it seemed the family's troubles would come to an end. John rode to Palmyra to be sworn in and, while returning home, was drenched by a cold storm. Pneumonia soon developed, the doctors came and went, but he grew weaker. "On the morning of the 24th of March, 1847, it was evident that he could not live many hours. He was very weak . . . . A little later he beckoned to Pamela, now a lovely girl of nineteen, and, putting his arm about her neck, kissed her for the first time in years. 'Let me die,' he said. He never spoke after that. The sad, weary life that had lasted less than forty-nine years was ended: A dreamer and a moralist, an upright man honored by all, he had never been a financier. He ended life with less than he had begun" (Paine, Chapter 14).

Sam was 11 when his father died. The family needed money, so Sam was apprenticed to Joseph P. Ament, owner of the *Missouri Courier*, to learn the printing trade. Albert Paine, biographer, says, "When he had been with Ament little more than a year Sam had become office favorite and chief standby. Whatever required intelligence and care and imagination was given to Sam Clemens . . . . He became a sort of subeditor" (Chapter 15).

One of the most transforming incidents in Sam Clemens' life occurred when he found a single page of a history book while on his way home from work. The sheet fluttered along, he caught it, and discovered it was from a history book describing the imprisonment of Joan of Arc, the Maid of Orleans. Paine says, "It meant the awakening of his interest in all history—the world's story in its many phases—a passion which became the largest feature of his intellectual life and remained with him until his very last day on earth. From the moment when that fluttering leaf was blown into his hands, his career as one of the world's mentally elect was assured. It gave him his cue—the first word of a part in the human drama."

Written on cloth to the left of the daguerreotype: Samuel L Clemens, likeness taken
Dec 1850, Age 15. Cross-written in pencil: Taken in December 1850—age 15.
On the paper lining underneath the picture, in pencil:
GH Jones, Hannibal—Mo 1850, Nov 29th

In this image of Samuel Clemens, he is holding metal type, which he
cleverly positioned backwards to compensate for the mirror-image
rendered by the camera. Both images courtesy of the Mark Twain Project—
The Bancroft Library, University of California, Berkeley,

17

Twain began a passionate study of history that would continue for the rest of his life and he would become one of the most well-read and intellectually literate people in America or the world (Paine, Chapter 16).

Orion returned to Hannibal from St. Louis and decided, after borrowing a $500 mortgage, to buy the *Hannibal Journal* with visions of making it a financial success. Sam, now trained in the printing trade, was hired to work for the paper, but Sam never saw much money. Paine relates, "Those were hard financial days. Orion could pay nothing on his mortgage—barely the interest. He had promised Sam three dollars and a half a week, but he could do no more than supply him with board and clothes—'poor, shabby clothes,' Twain says in his record" (Paine, Chapter 18).

When Orion made a trip to Tennessee, Sam was left in charge of the office and decided to write more satirical articles to liven up the paper. He wrote a scathing article about a rival editor who tried to drown himself after losing his love, including an engraving showing the man walking into the river with a measuring stick. It was hugely successful and the paper had to run extra copies to keep up with demand. Orion was not amused when he returned, but Sam had found his calling. "Seeing them in print was a joy which rather exceeded anything in that line I have ever experienced since," Sam said, nearly sixty years later. Paine notes, "He had got his first taste of print, and he liked it. He promptly wrote two anecdotes which he thought humorous and sent them to the Philadelphia *Saturday Evening Post*. They were accepted—without payment, of course, in those days; and when the papers containing them appeared he felt suddenly lifted to a lofty plane of literature" (Paine, Chapter 18).

Sam stayed with the paper for years, but in 1853 at 18 years of age, he left Hannibal, his brother Orion, and his mother Jane, after promising her he would never drink liquor or play cards.

He traveled to St. Louis, New York, Philadephia, and Cincinnati, working as a typesetter, but remained unsettled and without a future. He finally decided to head for the Amazon River and South America to invest in cocoa and took passage on the *Paul Jones*, a steamboat piloted by Horace Bixby, a legendary pilot on the Mississippi, to reach New Orleans. Sam looked up at the pilothouse, and his old boyhood dreams, and almost every other boy's dreams, of becoming a river boat pilot made him change his mind about traveling to the Amazon (Paine, Chapter 22).

"OUR PERMANENT AMBITION."

Illustration from Mark Twain's *Life on the Mississippi*

As Twain relates in *Life on the Mississippi*:

> When I was a boy, there was but one permanent ambition among my comrades in our village on the west bank of the Mississippi River. That was to be a steamboatman. We had transient ambitions of other sorts, but they were only transient . . . . When a circus came and went, it left us all burning to become

clowns, the first negro minstrel show that ever came to our section left us all suffering to try that kind of life; now and then we had a hope that, if we lived and were good, God would permit us to be pirates. These ambitions faded out, each in its turn; but the ambition to be a steamboatman always remained. (Chapter 4)

"BESEIGING THE PILOT."

Illustration from Mark Twain's *Life on the Mississippi*

Sam was personable, funny, bright, very good company, and he made friends easily wherever he went, which might explain why Bixby finally agreed to take him on a as a cub pilot, after days of Sam's pleading. Paine states, "Something about this young man had won Horace Bixby's heart. His slow, pleasant speach; his unhurried, quiet manner with the wheel, his evident sincerity of purpose—these were externals, but beneath them the pilot felt something of that quality of mind or heart which later made the world love Mark Twain" (Chapter 22).

BECOMING A PILOT

Soon, Bixby let Sam take the wheel and rattled off an endless list of commands, points, stumps, bends, snags, whirlpools and other information about the river that Sam would have to remember. When asked to recall these items at the end of his watch, Sam was clueless and without memory. Bixby told him,

> My boy, you must get a little memorandum book, and every time I tell you a thing put it down right away. There's only one way to be a pilot, and that is to get this entire river by heart. You have to know it just like ABC.

So Sam Clemens got the little book, and presently it "fairly bristled" with the names of towns, point, bars, islands, bends and reaches. But it made his heart ache to think that he had only half of the river set down; for, as the "watches" were four hours off and four hours on, there were long gaps during which he had slept (Paine, Chapter 23).

And that is how the notebooks got started. Later on, "Notebook Number Four," with accounting of Twain's adventures out West, would begin many miles and memories away from the Mississippi River.

"LEARNING THE RIVER."

Illustration from Mark Twain's *Life on the Mississippi*

For the next two years, Sam studied the 1,200 miles of the Mississippi River, which he had to learn to navigate. Sam always observed the character and personality of all the pilots he worked with. Some pilots, like Bixby, were kind, considerate, and helpful in teaching their young protégées. Others, like William Brown, made the cub pilots' lives a misery. Sam describes the wretched and insufferable treatment Brown gave to his cub pilots in *Life on the Mississippi*:

> He was a middle-aged, long, slim, bony, smooth-shaven, horse-faced, ignorant, stingy, malicious, snarling, fault-finding, mote-magnifying tyrant. I early got the habit of coming on watch with dread at my heart.
>
> I often wanted to kill Brown, but this would not

answer. A cub had to take everything his boss gave, in the way of vigorous comment and criticism; and we all believed that there was a United States law making it a penitentiary offense to strike or threaten a pilot. However, I could imagine myself killing Brown; there was no law against that and that was the thing I used always to do the moment I was abed . . . . I killed Brown every night for months; not in old, stale, commonplace ways, but in new and picturesque ones—ways that were sometimes surprising for freshness of design and ghastliness of situation and environments.

Brown was always watching for a pretext to find fault; and if he could find no plausible pretext, he would invent one. He would scold you for shaving a shore, and for not shaving it; for hugging a bar, and for not hugging it; for "pulling down" when not invited, and for not pulling down when not invited; for firing up without orders, and for waiting for orders. In a word, it was his invariable rule to find fault with everything you did. (*Life on the Mississippi*, Chapter 18)

Luckily, Sam was not alone, as he encouraged his younger brother Henry to join him on the river. Sam was very close to Henry and thought that the best thing he could do for him was to get him out of the family home and onto the river to become a pilot also. As Paine tells it, "Henry Clemens was about twenty at this time, a handsome, attractive boy of whom his brother was lavishly fond and proud. He did go on the next trip and continued to go regularly after that, as third clerk in line of promotion. It was a bright spot in those hard days with Brown to have Henry along. The boys spent a good deal of their leisure with the other pilot, George Ealer, 'who was as

Portrait of Sam's brother, Henry Clemens
Photo courtesy of the Mark Twain Project—
The Bancroft Library,
University of California, Berkeley

kindhearted as Brown wasn't,' and quoted Shakespeare and Goldsmith, and played the flute to his fascinated and inspiring audience" (Paine, Chapter 25).

One day while Brown was at the wheel with Sam standing by, Henry delivered a message to Brown from Captain John Kleinfelter that would change the course of Sam's life forever:

> Somewhere down the river (it was Eagle Bend) Henry appeared on the hurricane deck to bring an order from the captain for a landing to be made a little lower down. Brown was somewhat deaf, but would never confess it. He may not have understood the order; at all events he gave no sign of having heard it, and went straight ahead. He disliked Henry as he disliked everybody of finer grain than himself, and in any case was too arrogant to ask for a repetition. They were passing the landing when Captain Kleinfelter appeared on deck and called to him to let the boat come around, adding:
>
> "Didn't Henry tell you to land here?"
>
> "No sir."

Captain Kleinfelter turned to Sam:

"Didn't you hear him?"

"Yes, sir."

Brown said: "Shut your mouth! You never heard anything of the kind" (Paine, Chapter 25).

The cub pilot, Sam, had virtually called Brown a liar in front of the Captain. Something had to give.

By and by Henry came into the pilot-house, unaware any trouble. Brown set upon him in his ugliest manner.

"Here, why didn't you tell me we had got to land at that plantation?" he demanded.

Henry was always polite, always gentle.

"I did tell you, Mr. Brown."

"It's a lie."

Sam Clemens could stand Brown's abuse of himself, but not of Henry. He said "You lie yourself. He did tell you."

Brown was dazed for a moment and then he shouted:

"I'll attend to your case in half a minute!" and ordered Henry out of the pilot-house." (Paine, Chapter 25)

But, for Henry and Sam, life would be forever altered before Henry got through that door.

The boy started out, and even had his foot on the upper step outside the door, when Brown with a sudden access of fury, picked up a ten pound lump of

"I HIT BROWN A GOOD HONEST BLOW."

Illustration from Mark Twain's *Life on the Mississippi*

coal and sprang after him; but I was between, with a heavy stool, and I hit Brown with a good honest blow which stretched him out...I stuck to him and pounded him with my fists a considerable time. I do not know how long, the pleasure of it probably made it seem longer than it really was; but in the end he struggled free and jumped up and sprang to the wheel: a very natural solicitude, for, all this time, here was the steamboat tearing down the river at the rate of fifteen miles an hour and nobody at the helm! (*Life on the Mississippi*, Chapter 19)

Sam was ordered out of the pilot-house and knew his fate, he'd go to jail and could forget his dreams of becoming a pilot. But Kleinfelter would have none of that. He took Sam to his cabin and asked him to carefully describe what happened in every detail, finally asking, "Did you pound him much, that is, severely?" Sam replied, "One might call it that, sir, maybe." To Sam's amazement, the captain said he was "deuced glad of it! Hark ye, never mention that I said that. You have been guilty of a great crime: and don't you ever be guilty of it again. But—lay for him ashore! Give him a good sound thrashing, do you hear? I'll pay the expenses." Sam said, "I slid out, happy with the sense of a close shave, and a mighty deliverance; and I heard him laughing to himself and slapping his fat thighs after I had closed the door." Brown refused to work with Sam ever again, and Kleinfelter found him another berth on the *A.T. Lacey* (*Life on the Mississippi*, Chapter 19).

The brothers stayed together in New Orleans until the *Pennsylvania* left upriver with Brown at the wheel and Henry on board, followed two days later by Sam on the *A.T. Lacey*. "We touched at Greenville, Mississippi, a couple of days out and somebody shouted:

"HENRY AND I SAT CHATTING."

Illustration from Mark Twain's *Life on the Mississippi*

'The Pennsylvania is blown up at Ship Island, and a hundred and fifty lives lost!' " The first news Sam heard was that Henry was not hurt, but later, Henry was listed as "hurt beyond help" (*Life on the Mississippi*, Chapter 20).

Twain describes the carnage of the disaster:

> Ealer rang to "come ahead" full steam, and the next moment four of the eight boilers exploded with a thunderous crash, and the whole forward third of the boat was hoisted toward the sky! . . . Brown, the pilot, and George Black, chief clerk, were never seen or heard of after the explosion. The barber's chair, with Captain Kleinfelter in it and unhurt, was left with its back overhanging vacancy—everything forward of it, floor and all, had disappeared; and the stupefied barber . . . stood with one toe projecting over space, still stirring his lather unconsciously and saying not a word . . . By this time the fire was making fierce headway . . . All efforts to conquer the fire proved fruitless. (*Life on the Mississippi*, Chapter 20)

Henry, whose room was directly above the boilers, was blown through the ceiling by the scalding steam. He fell back on top of the boilers and crawled off the burning boat. He was picked up by a rescue boat and taken to a makeshift hospital in Memphis. Sam showed up one day later, and he describes the terrible agony of watching his brother die:

> Forty of the wounded were placed upon pallets on the floor of the great public hall, and among these was Henry . . . The sight I saw when I entered that hall was new and strange to me. Two long rows of prostrate forms—more than forty in all—and every face and head a shapeless wad of loose raw

THE EXPLOSION.

Illustration from Mark Twain's *Life on the Mississippi*

cotton. It was a gruesome spectacle. I watched there six days and nights, and a very melancholy experience it was . . . . Dr. Peyton, a principal physician, and rich in all the attributes that go to constitute high and flawless character, did all that educated judgment and trained skill could do for Henry; but, as the newspapers had said in the beginning, his hurts were past help. On the evening of the sixth day his wandering mind busied itself with matters far away, and his nerveless fingers "picked at his coverlet." His hour had struck; we bore him to the death-room, poor boy. (*Life on the Mississippi*, Chapter 20)

Paine relates a letter Sam was able to compose to Mollie Clemens, Orion's wife, after days of caring for Henry: "Long before this reaches you my poor Henry—my darling, my pride, my glory, my all will have finished his blameless career, and the light of my life will have gone out in utter darkness. The horrors of three days have swept over me—they have blasted my youth and left me an old man before my time."

Paine wrote, "In many ways he never overcame the tragedy of Henry's death. He never really looked young again. Gray hairs had come, as he said, and they did not disappear. His face took on the serious, pathetic look which from that time it always had in repose. At twenty-three he looked thirty. At thirty he looked nearer forty.

After that the discrepancy in age and looks became less notable. In vigor, complexion, and temperament he was regarded in later life as young for his years, but never in looks" (Paine, Chapter 26). This was one of the many tragic events that occured during Mark Twain's life and, like so many others, one for which he felt completely responsible.

THE HOSPITAL WARD.

Illustration from Mark Twain's *Life on the Mississippi*

Clemens' pilot license was granted on September 9, 1857, and Paine would write about this extraordinary accomplishment:

> He was a pilot at last. In eighteen months he had packed away in his head all the multitude of volatile statistics and acquired that confidence and courage which made him one of the elect, a river sovereign. He knew every snag and band and dead tree and reef in all those endless miles between St. Louis and New Orleans, every cut-off and current, every depth of water—the whole story—by night and by day. He could smell danger in the dark; he could read the surface of the water as an open page. At twenty-three he had acquired a profession which surpassed all others for absolute sovereignty and yielded an income equal to that then earned by the Vice-President of the United States. Boys generally finish college at about that age, but it is not likely that any boy ever finished college with the mass of practical information and training that was stored away in Samuel Clemens's head, or with his knowledge of human nature, his preparation for battle with the world. (Paine, Chapter 27)

And according to Horace Bixby, he was a good pilot.

> Sam Clemens never had an accident either as a steersman or as a pilot, except once when he got aground for a few hours in the bagasse (cane) smoke, with no damage to anybody; though of course there was some good luck in that too, for the best pilots do not escape trouble, now and then. (Paine, Chapter 28)

Mark Twain would say, "I loved the profession far better than any I have followed since," and long afterward declared, "I took a

'LET A LEADSMAN CRY, "'HALF TWAIN.'"

Illustration from Mark Twain's *Life on the Mississippi*

measureless pride in it." As Paine states, "The dreamy, easy, romantic existence suited him exactly. A sovereign and an autocrat, the pilot's word was law; he wore his responsibilities as a crown. As long as he lived Samuel Clemens would return to those old days with fondness and affection, and with regret that they were no more" (Paine, Chapter 29).

It would take an unnatural force to remove Sam from the river and, unfortunately for him, the election of Lincoln in 1860 and the coming of the Civil War was just that kind of calamity for him, and the country.

CIVIL WAR AND TIME TO SKEDADDLE

Sam was a passenger on the *Uncle Sam* making his way north to find work when he witnessed the closing of the Mississsippi River at the start of the Civil War.

> He went up the river as a passenger on a steamer named the *Uncle Sam*. Zeb Leavenworth was one of the pilots, and Sam Clemens usually stood watch with him . . . . Abreast of Jefferson Barracks they suddenly heard the boom of a cannon and saw a great whorl of smoke drifting in their direction. They did not realize that it was a signal—a thunderous halt—and kept straight on. Less than a minute later there was another boom, and a shell exploded directly in front of the pilot-house, breaking a lot of glass and destroying a good deal of the upper decoration. Zeb Leavenworth fell back into a corner with a yell.
>
> "Good Lord Almighty! Sam," he said, "what do they mean by that?"
>
> Clemens stepped to the wheel and brought the boat around. "I guess they want us to wait a minute,

HIS MAIDEN BATTLE.

Illustration from Mark Twain's *Life on the Mississippi*

Zeb," he said.

They were examined and passed. It was the last steamboat to make the trip from New Orleans to St. Louis. Mark Twain's pilot-days were over. He would have grieved had he known this fact. (Paine, Chapter 29)

Unlike millions of other young American men who were drawn into the bloodshed and carnage of the Civil War, Sam Clemens had a way out. Orion worked to get Lincoln elected and was rewarded for his efforts by being given an appoint-ment to the post of Secretary of the new Nevada Territory. Sam saw his chance to absquatulate and skedaddle, as he put it, from the forthcoming horrors of the war. Orion would give him the title of sec-retary to the Secretary, and Sam would use his savings to pay for their trip to Nevada (Paine, Chapter 31).

Orion Clemens,
Photo courtesy of the
Mark Twain Project—
The Bancroft Library,
University of California,
Berkeley

The brothers left in July, 1861, and af-ter twenty days of traveling across Ameri-ca, they arrived in Carson City, a trip Mark Twain later retold in *Roughing It* (1872):

We resumed undress uniform, climbed a-top of the flying coach, dangled our legs over the side, shouted occasionally at our frantic mules, merely to see them lay their ears back and scamper faster, tied our hats on to keep our hair from blowing away, and leveled an outlook over the world-wide carpet about us for new and strange things to gaze at. Even to this day it thrills me through and through to think of the life, the gladness and the wild sense of freedom that

OUR MORNING RIDE.

Illustration from Mark Twain's *Roughing It*

used to make the blood dance in my veins on those
fine overland mornings. (*Roughing It*, Chapter 5)

After Sam arrived in Carson City, he soon discovered there really was no job as secretary to the Secretary, and he would have to
try his hand at earning a living. He was staying in a rooming house
with a band of men he would call the "Irish Brigade" and was, as
Paine wrote, "interested more in the native riches above ground than
in those concealed under it. He had heard that the timber around
Lake Bigler (Tahoe) promised vast wealth which could be had for the
asking. The lake itself and the adjacent mountains were said to be
beautiful beyond the dream of art. He decided to locate a timber

claim on its shores." With a new partner, Johnny K, he agreed to make the trip to the timber stand and set up the claim (Paine, Chapter 32).

They had no horse, and after miles and hours of aimless wanderings, found the top of the last ridge where, as he describes in Chapter 22 of *Roughing It*:

> We plodded on, two or three hours longer, and at last, the lake burst upon us—a noble sheet of blue water lifted 6,300 feet above the level of the sea and walled in by a rim of snow-clad mountain peaks that towered aloft full three thousand feet higher . . . As it lay there with the shadows of the mountains brilliantly photographed upon its still surface, I thought it must surely be the fairest picture the whole earth affords . . . We liked the appearance of the place and stuck our "notices" on a tree . . . If there is any life that

Vista of Lake Tahoe today by Mariusz Blach

is happier than the life we led on our timber ranch for the next two or three weeks, it must be a sort of life which I have not read of in books or experienced in person.

They were, in fact, property owners and wealthy men. The timber was desperately needed in the mines of the Comstock, and Sam's future was secure. He dreamed of great wealth and a comfortable, glorious life on the lake. After several tranquil, wonderful weeks of discovery, provisions began to run out and they had to return to Carson City to record the claim and resupply after one more perfect night on the lakeshore. As Sam retells it, [he]—

> . . . lit a fire and went back to the boat to get the frying pan. I heard a shout from Johnny and looking up I saw that my fire was galloping all over the premises! In a minute and a half, the fire seized upon a dense growth of dry manzanita chaparral six or eight feet high, and then the roaring and popping and crackling was something terrific. We sat absorbed and motionless through four long hours. We were homeless wanderers again without any property. (*Roughing It*, Chapter 23)

They returned to Carson City and informed the brigade they had no timber, no timber claim on Lake Tahoe, and had lost their fortune. Sam failed at every job and mining adventure he undertook.

In *Roughing It*, he said he was too slow as a typesetter, failed as a private secretary, grocery clerk, blacksmith, prospector, silver miner, Tahoe timber owner, quartz mine laborer, and finally, he recounted:

> I did what many and many a poor disappointed miner had done before; said it was all over with me now and I will never go back home to be pitied—and snubbed. I had been a private secretary, a silver miner,

FIRE AT LAKE TAHOE.

Illustration from Mark Twain's *Roughing It*

a silver mill operative and amounted to less than nothing in each case and now, what to do next? . . . .

Now in pleasanter days I had amused myself with writing letters to the chief paper of the Territory, the Virginia *Daily Territorial Enterprise*, and was always surprised when they appeared in print . . . . I had found a letter in the post office as I came home from the hillside, and finally I opened it. Eureka! . . . . It was a deliberate offer to me of Twenty-Five Dollars a week to come up to Virginia City and be city editor of the Enterprise . . . . Twenty Five Dollars a week—it looked like bloated luxury—a fortune—a sinful and lavish waste of money. (*Roughing It*, Chapter 42)

WORTH NOTHING.

Illustration from *Mark Twain's Roughing It*

But why would Sam, an unknown and unheard of miner or writer, be hired by Joe Goodman, the owner of the *Territorial Enterprise*? George Williams III retells the story of how Sam came to work for the *Enterprise* in his book *Mark Twain: His Life in Virginia City, Nevada:*

> Shortly after arriving in Aurora, Clemens began writing humorous letters about the trials and tribulations of a hard-luck miner. Clemens signed the letters "Josh" and sent them to the Territorial Enterprise in Virginia City where they were published. Editor Joe Goodman was impressed by the "Josh" letters and thought the writer was worth cultivating. Goodman was looking for someone to replace Dan De Quille in the autumn as local editor while De Quille visited family back East. "Josh" seemed like a likely replacement. In late July, Goodman asked William Barstow, his business manager, to write Clemens and offer him a job as local reporter (16).

Sam was wearing the alkali-covered, wretched clothes, the only ones he had, when he walked into the *Territorial Enterprise* office in September, 1862. He'd walked 130 miles across the desert from Aurora, Nevada, sometimes at night. Paine would write, "He wore a rusty slouch hat, no coat, a faded blue flannel shirt, a Navy revolver; his trousers were hanging on his boot tops. A tangle of reddish-brown hair fell on his shoulders, and a mass of tawny beard, dingy with alkali dust, dropped half-way to his waist." Anything but an impressive sight. But, when he introduced himself to office staff, he was warmly received, especially by Dan De Quille who admired the "Josh" letters and thought Clemens worth training as a newspaper writer (Paine, Chap. 37).

AS CITY EDITOR.

Illustration from Mark Twain's *Roughing It*

THE GILLIS CLAN

Also on the staff was Steve Gillis, foreman of the *Enterprise* composing room and a very respected newspaper man. The Gillis clan, three brothers—Steve, Jim, and Billy—arrived in California by way of the Mexican War, led by their father, Major Angus Gillis, who was, as Twain wrote in his *Autobiography*—

> . . . in the memorable Plaza fight and stood it out to the last against overwhelming odds . . . The son was killed at the father's side. The father received a bullet through the eye. The old man—for he was an old man at the time—wore spectacles, and the bullet and one of the glasses went into his skull, and the bullet remained there.

Clemens, who later boarded with Angus from time to time in San Francisco, recounted that when Angus became too emotional, he shed tears and glass alike, a courage and bravery Sam found remarkable in all the Gillis men (Chapter 23).

Steve's brothers, William (Billy) and Jim, lived with Dick Stoker in a cabin on Jackass Hill where Sam would later stay for those memorable 88 days. Remembrances and recollections of Sam's experiences with the Gillis clan were written by brother Billy in two books, *Goldrush Days with Mark Twain* and *Memories of Mark Twain and Steve Gillis*, both treasure troves of stories about Sam's adventures in the West. Billy describes Steve and Sam's first encounter:

> With one of his hearty laughs, Steve started, with extended hand, across the room, saying,
>
> "Why, Mr. Clemens, I am surely glad to see you, although you don't look a bit like the Sam Clemens pictured in my mind."

"Why Mr. Gillis," said Sam, "I don't often cotton to a man on first acquaintance, but I do cotton to you, right here and now, and I know that we're going to be friends right from the start." And so it proved to be. There was never a truer or closer friendship between two people than that between Sam and Steve. (*Goldrush Days*, 48)

Sam would eventually be forced to leave Virginia City and Nevada for the safer and more cosmopolitan world of San Francisco, with Steve Gillis riding along in the same stagecoach.

THE TERRITORIAL ENTERPRISE

Joe Goodman was the newspaper's brilliant owner/editor who admired Sam's stories, but he knew the paper was taking a terrible risk. Sam had to learn how to become a reporter and columnist and to come up with two columns of stories (over 2,000 words) every day in a manner befitting the paper. *Enterprise* writers like Joe Goodman, Dan De Quille, Jim Townsend, Rollin Daggett (aka *The Merciless,* "who wasn't content to shred a victim, but preferred to annihilate the subject of scorn") had established the finest newspaper on the West Coast. It was recognized for its

Joe Goodman, photo courtesy of the Nevada Historical Society

honor, integrity, and ruthless persecution of any perceived injustice, and there was plenty of dishonor and injustice in Virginia City (Williams, *Virginia City*, 48).

Sam had to prove himself to these men and the ever constant pressure and need to produce stories would get him in trouble from time to time.

Goodman would later say it was De Quille who taught Sam how to write for the paper, and he thought De Quille to be the better writer.

> If I had been asked to prophesy which of the two men, Dan De Quille or Sam, would become distinguished, I should have said De Quille. Dan was talented, industrious, and, for that time and place, brilliant. Of course, I recognized the unusualness of Sam's gifts, but he was eccentric and seemed to lack industry; it is not likely that I should have prophesied fame for him then. (Paine, Chapter 39)

Composing room of the Territorial Enterprise in Virginia City, Nevada
Photo courtesy of the Nevada Historical Society.

One of Sam's outstanding characteristics and a major contributor to his success was his natural ability to be comfortable with people and make friends easily. George Williams III notes in his *Mark Twain: His Life in Virginia City, Nevada*:

> Clemens was a human magnet and drew people to him naturally. He did not have to work to get the attention of others. Joe Goodman said, "Back in the old days, Sam was the best company, the drollest entertainer and the most interesting fellow imaginable. His humor was always cropping out ..." Those who knew Clemens best said his speech was funnier than his writing. Clemens would tell humorous stories for hours while an enraptured gathering laughed till their sides ached and time seemed to pass quickly. Clemens loved being the center of attention and he was skillful in the ways he achieved it. He was a ham, an actor, a born entertainer. He enjoyed people, enjoyed himself and loved making people laugh and feel good. (Williams, *Virginia City*, 71)

Virginia City was witness to the greatest eruption of wealth west of the Mississippi, the Comstock Lode, which would produce over $20 million in silver beginning in 1863, and the city would boom to a population of over 20,000 with Sam right in the middle of it all.

Anyone famous visiting the West would travel through Virginia City, which is what Artemus Ward, America's greatest writing and stage humorist at the time, would do in December, 1863. Ward was only two years older than Sam, but rich on a national and international level, and made a fortune doing what he loved to do best—present his special brand of humor on the stage. And as Paine later observed, "There was a fine opera-house in Virginia, and any attraction that billed San Francisco did not fail to play to the

Virginia City 1865, courtesy of the Nevada Historical Society

Comstock. Ward intended staying only a few days to deliver his lectures, but the whirl of the Comstock caught him like a maelstrom, and he remained three weeks" (Paine, Chapter 43).

Goodman, Clemens, and Dan De Quille were responsible for hosting Ward during his anticipated three-day stay. Ward liked the company of these men and their desire to indulge in endless, drunken celebrations of one kind or another, and added 11 days to his stay to continue their legendary revelries through day and night. There was great mutual admiration and respect between Ward and the soon-to-be-famous Clemens—enough respect that Ward used his enormous influence to convince the New York *Sunday Mercury* to print two of Sam's stories in February, 1864. He would also ask Sam to send along a story later in the year, a story Ward would include in his own book of tales and adventures in the West (Paine, Chapter 44).

Albert Paine describes the importance of the relationship between Artemis Ward and Mark Twain, one that would influence Twain for the rest of his life:

> He (Ward) made the *Enterprise* office his headquarters, and fairly reveled in the company he found there. He and Mark Twain became boon companions. Each recognized in the other a kindred spirit. With Goodman, De Quille, and McCarthy, also E. E. Hingston—Ward's agent, a companionable fellow— they usually dined at Chaumond's, Virginia's high-toned French restaurant.
>
> Those were three memorable weeks in Mark Twain's life. Artemus Ward was in the height of his fame, and he encouraged his new-found brother-humorist and prophesied great things of him. Clemens, on his side, measured himself by this man who had achieved fame, and perhaps with good reason concluded that Ward's estimate was correct, that he too could win fame and honor, once he got a start. (Paine, Chapter 43)

Ward's lecture, entitled "Babes in the Wood," wasn't a lecture at all but a commentary on a wide variety of subjects, all of immediate interest or knowledge to his audience, and he knew his audience well. Clemens noted how hard Ward worked to understand miners, their lives, their troubles, and the nature of life in Virginia City so he could interject all manner of commentary in his program. Miners loved and adored Artemus Ward, and he loved them right back.

Sam would write a review of Ward's performance and note, "The man who is capable of listening to the 'Babes in the Wood' from beginning to end without laughing either inwardly or outwardly must have done murder, or at least meditated on it, at some time during his life" (qtd. in Williams, *Virginia City*, 126).

SAM CLEMENS FINDS A NEW NAME

According to Paine, the name Mark Twain, "was first signed to a Carson letter bearing the date of February 2, 1863, and from that time was attached to all Samuel Clemens' work." He'd worked for the *Enterprise* for about five months, and Goodman's allowing the use of a pen name was an important honor. Only the most important, respected, or well-known reporters had real or pen names identifying their writings, and these names became familiar with all the paper's readers. Goodman must have decided Sam was now a successful, established writer and could use his own pen name, Mark Twain (Paine, Chapter 40).

When asked about how he chose the name, Twain would connect it to a river pilot he knew many years ago on the Mississippi, Captain Isaiah Sellers. Sellers was the dean of river pilots, having served longer than any other, and Twain described him in Chapter 50 of *Life on the Mississippi*:

> He was a fine man, a high-minded man, and greatly respected, both ashore and on the river. He was very tall, well built, and handsome, and in his old age—as I remember him—his hair was as black as an Indian's, and his eye and hand were as strong and steady and his nerve and judgements firm and clear as anybody's, young or old, among the fraternity of pilots. He was the patriarch of the craft . . .

> The old gentleman was not of literary turn or capacity, but he used to jot down brief paragraphs of plain, practical information about the river and sign them "Mark Twain," and give them to the New Orleans *Picayune*.

Sam was just a cub pilot back then, but he took it upon himself to write a satirical "burlesque," as he called it, of some 800 words which appeared in the *True Delta*, his very first published article of writing. It was a disaster. He simply had no idea how his personally directed sarcasm would humiliate a respected man who was powerless to know what to do about it. Sam would later write:

> There was no malice in my rubbish; but it laughed at the captain. It laughed at a man to whom such a thing was new and strange and dreadful. I did not know then, though I do now, that there is no suffering comparable with that which a private person feels when he is for the first time pilloried in print. (*Life on the Mississippi*, Chapter 50)

Sellers would never write another paragraph, nor forgive the cub pilot who wrote the article.

Paine retells this story about Mark Twain's name origin in his biography:

> "Joe," he said, to Goodman, "I want to sign my articles. I want to be identified to a wider audience."
>
> "All right, Sam. What name do you want to use 'Josh'?"
>
> "No, I want to sign them 'Mark Twain.' It is an old river term, a leads-man's call, signifying two fathoms—twelve feet. It has a richness about it; it was always a pleasant sound for a pilot to hear on a dark night; it meant safe water."
>
> He did not then mention that Captain Isaiah Sellers had used and dropped the name. He was ashamed of his part in that episode, and the offense was still too recent for confession. Goodman considered a moment:

"Very well, Sam," he said, "that sounds like a good name."

As Paine notes, it was indeed a good name.

> In all the nomenclature of the world no more forceful combination of words could have been selected to express the man for whom they stood. The name Mark Twain is as infinite, as fundamental as that of John Smith, without the latter's wasting distribution of strength. If all the prestige in the name of John Smith were combined in a single individual, its dynamic energy might give it the carrying power of Mark Twain. Let this be as it may, it has proven the greatest 'nom de plume' ever chosen—a name exactly in accord with the man, his work, and his career. (Paine, Chapter 40)

George Williams III includes a letter Mark wrote to the *Alta California* published on June 9, 1877, about the source of his name:

> "Mark Twain" was the nom de plume of one Captain Isaiah Sellers, who used to write river news over it for the New Orleans *Picayune*. He died in 1863 and as he could no longer need that signature, I laid violent hands upon it without asking permission of the proprietor's remains. That is the history of the nom de plume I bear. (qtd. in Williams, *Virginia City*, 93)

Williams also notes Sellers never signed the name Mark Twain and offers another legendary tale presented by George W. Cassidy, a newspaper man in Virginia City, who claimed the name originated in John Piper's bar, the Old Corner Saloon:

> John Piper's saloon on B Street used to be the grand rendezvous for all the Virginia City Bohemians. Piper conducted a cash business and refused to keep

MARK TWAIN'S 88 DAYS IN THE MOTHER LODE

any books. As a special favor, however, he would occasionally chalk down drinks to the boys, on the wall
back of the bar. Sam, when localizing for the *Enterprise*, always had an account, with the balance against
him on Piper's wall. Clemens was by no means a Coal
Oil Tommy—he drank for the pure and unadulter-
ated love of the ardent. Most of his drinking was
conducted in single-handed contests, but occasionally he would invite Dan De Quille, Charley Parker,
Bob Lowery, or Alf Doten—never more than one
of them, however, at time, and whenever he did,
his invariable parting injunction to Piper was to
"Mark Twain" meaning two chalk marks, of course.
(Williams, *Virginia City*, 96)

Whether its origin was a reference to "safe water," Captain
Seller's pen name, or to what was written in chalk on Piper's wall,
Mark Twain would become one of the most famous names in the
history of American literature.

THE DUEL

Joe Goodman had to leave Virginia City for a short time and left
Sam in editoral charge of the paper, which proved to be a mistake.
Sam took it upon himself to write personally directed criticisms at
individuals and newspapers who he thought didn't do enough in
contributing to a very special fundraiser, the "Flour Sack Fund." The
fund was going to help an organization, later called the Red Cross,
that assisted soldiers wounded during the war.

As Paine relates:

In the general hilarity of this occasion, certain
Enterprise paragraphs of criticism or ridicule had
incurred the displeasure of various individuals whose
cause naturally enough had been espoused by a

54

"C" Street, Virginia City, NV in 1865, looking north from Taylor Street—Courtesy of the Mark Twain Project—The Bancroft Library, University of California, Berkeley

rival paper, the *Chronicle*. Very soon the original grievance, whatever it was, was lost sight of in the fireworks and vitriol-throwing of personal recrimination between Mark Twain and the *Chronicle* editor, then a Mr. Laird. A point had been reached at length when only a call for bloodshed—a challenge— could satisfy either the staff or the readers of the two papers. Men were killed every week for milder things than the editors had spoken, each of the other. (Paine, Chapter 45)

The level of anger escalated, and Sam, encouraged by Steve Gillis and the rest of the *Enterprise* staff, challenged Laird to a duel. Paine retells the story of Sam Clemens' very first duel and makes special note that the account is from Steve Gillis' own hand:

. . . I helped Mark get up some of the letters, and a man who would not fight after such letters did not belong in Virginia City—in those days.

Laird's acceptance of Mark's challenge came along about midnight, I think, after the papers had gone to press. The meeting was to take place next morning at sunrise.

Of course I was selected as Mark's second, and at daybreak I had him up and out for some lessons in pistol practice before meeting Laird. I didn't have to wake him. He had not been asleep. We had been talking since midnight over the duel that was coming. I had been telling him of the different duels in which I had taken part, either as principal or second, and how many men I had helped to kill and bury, and how it was a good plan to make a will, even if one had not much to leave. It always looked well, I told him, and seemed to be a proper thing to do before going into a duel.

So Mark made a will with a sort of gloomy satisfaction, and as soon as it was light enough to see, we went out to a little ravine near the meeting-place, and I set up a board for him to shoot at. He would step out, raise that big pistol, and when I would count three he would shut his eyes and pull the trigger. Of course he didn't hit anything; he did not come anywhere near hitting anything. Just then we heard somebody shooting over in the next ravine. Sam said:

"What's that, Steve?"

"Why," I said, "that's Laird. His seconds are practicing him over there."

It didn't make my principal any more cheerful to hear that pistol go off every few seconds over there. Just then I saw a little mud-hen light on some sagebrush about thirty yards away.

"Mark," I said, "let me have that pistol. I'll show you how to shoot." He handed it to me, and I let go at the bird and shot its head off, clean. About that time Laird and his second came over the ridge to meet us. I saw them coming and handed Mark back the pistol. We were looking at the bird when they came up.

"Who did that?" asked Laird's second.

"Sam," I said.

"How far off was it?"

"Oh, about thirty yards."

"Can he do it again?"

"Of course," I said; "every time. He could do it twice that far."

Laird's second turned to his principal.

"Laird," he said, "you don't want to fight that man. It's just like suicide. You'd better settle this thing, now."

So there was a settlement. Laird took back all he had said; Mark said he really had nothing against Laird—the discussion had been purely journalistic and did not need to be settled in blood. He said that both he and Laird were probably the victims of their friends. I remember one of the things Laird said when his second told him he had better not fight.

> "Fight! H—l, no! I am not going to be murdered by that d—d desperado." (qtd. in Paine, Chapter 45)

Sam had also insulted and criticized a Mr. Cutler from Carson City who showed up in Virginia City and sent a man over from the hotel to the *Enterprise* office with a challenge for Sam. Sam sent Steve Gillis over to discuss the duel with Cutler.

> Steve went over to pacify him. Steve weighed only ninety-five pounds but it was well known throughout the territory that with his fists he could whip anybody that walked on two legs, let his weight and science be what they might.

> Steve was a Gillis, and when a Gillis confronted a man and had a proposition to make the proposition always contained business. When Cutler found that Steve was my second he cooled down; he became calm and rational and was ready to listen. Steve gave him fifteen minutes to get out of the hotel and half an hour to get out of town or there would be results. So that duel went off successfully, because Mr. Cutler immediately left for Carson a convinced and reformed man. (*Autobiography*, Chapter 23)

Two duels in one week, and a law had just been passed making dueling a penitentiary offense for both the principal and second. Jerry Driscoll, foreman of the Grand Jury, informed them they would either leave town the next day, or face prison. Steve said, "We concluded to go, and when the stage left next morning for San Francisco we were on the outside seat." Sam had worked for the *Enterprise,* the greatest newspaper on the West Coast, for 19 months and received an unparalleled education in journalism from the finest writers of his time who, each in his own way contributed to the legacy of Mark Twain (Paine, Chapter 46).

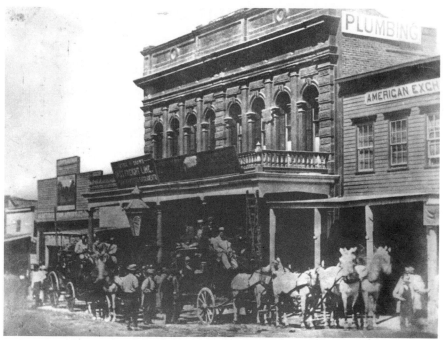

Wells Fargo Stage Coach, Virginia City, NV—Courtesy of the Mark Twain Project—
The Bancroft Library, University of California, Berkeley

TO SAN FRANCISCO

When Sam arrived in San Francisco, he was financially wealthy and lived a life he called "butterfly idleness." He had a trunk full of Gould and Curry stock which, like all other mining stocks in the West, continued to rise in value as speculators bought in a frenzy. Sam wrote, "I lived in the best hotels, exhibited my clothes in the most conspicuous places, infested the opera, and learned to seem enraptured wth music . . . . In a word, I kept the due state of a man worth a hundred thousand dollars" (*Roughing It*, Chapter 58).

He also found a young, vibrant, talented literary society, much like the men he left at the *Enterprise*. Paine describes the fresh, new writers who came to the West:

> More than any other city west of the Alleghanies,
> San Francisco has always been a literary center; and

certainly that was a remarkable group to be out there under the sunset, dropped down there behind the Sierras, which the transcontinental railway would not climb yet, for several years .... They felt that they were creating literature, as they were, in fact; a new school of American letters mustered there (Paine, Chapter 46).

And Bret Harte, editor of the *Californian*, would put Sam on the weekly payroll. Harte would be, for a short perod of time, more famous and familiar to Americans than Clemens after writing stories like "The Luck of Roaring Camp" (1868) and "The Outcasts of Poker Flat" (1869). He introduced Sam to his "Bohemian" culture and the many gifted writers and intellectuals who found their way to this free-wheeling city, which offered everything new and stimulating the East could not. As Paine would write, "With Mark Twain on the staff and Bret Harte in the chair, himself a frequent contributor, it easily ranked as first of San Francisco periodicals" (Paine, Chapter 46).

Of course for Sam Clemens, this kind of good fortune couldn't last. First, his Gould and Curry mining stock would crash.

> What a gambling carnival it was! Gould and Curry soared to six thousand three hundred dollars a foot! And then—all of a sudden, out went the bottom and everything and everybody went to ruin and destruction! The wreck was complete.

> The bubble scarcely left a microscopic moisture behind it. I was an early beggar and a thorough one. My hoarded stocks were not worth the paper they were printed on. (*Roughing It*, Chapter 58)

Sam found a new job as a reporter for the *Call* newspaper, in fact

DREAMS DISSIPATED.

Illustration from Mark Twain's *Roughing It*

the newspaper's only reporter, but found the work torturous. Paine writes, "Mark Twain's position on the *Call* was uncongenial from the start. San Francisco was a larger city than Virginia; the work there was necessarily more impersonal, more a routine of news-gathering and drudgery" (Chapter 47).

Twain would start at nine in the morning at the police court, cover the rest of the town, and visit as many as six theaters featuring plays and operas at night, and write out the days events and turn it in, perhaps very late at night (Paine, Chapter 47).

In his *Autobiography*, Twain describes his work for the *Call*:

> After having been hard at work from nine or ten in the morning until eleven at night scraping material together, I took the pen and spread this muck out in words and phrases and made it cover as much acreage as I could. It was fearful drudgery, soulless drudgery, and almost destitute of interest. It was awful slavery for a lazy man, and I was born lazy. I am no lazier now than I was at forty. (*Autobiography*, Chapter 24)

He would lose his job with the *Call*. Owner George Barnes would finally decide the time had come for them to part:

> Mr. Barnes discharged me. It was the only time in my life that I have been discharged and it hurts yet— although I am in my grave. He did not discharge me rudely. It was not in his nature to do that. He was a large, handsome man, with a kindly face and courteous ways, and faultless in his dress. He could not have said a rude, unsettled thing to anybody. He took me privately aside and advised me to resign. It was like a father advising a son for his good, and I obeyed. (*Autobiography*, Chapter 24)

Sam and Steve Gillis skipped from rooming house to rooming house because Sam was deeply in debt, his spirit completely broken:

> For two months my sole occupation was avoiding acquaintances; for during that time I did not earn a penny, or buy an article of any kind, or pay my board. I became very adept at "slinking." I slunk from back street to back street, I slunk away from approaching faces that looked familiar, I slunk to my meals, ate them humbly and with a mute apology for every mouthful I robbed my generous landlady of, and at midnight, after wanderings that were but slinkings away from cheerfulness and light, I slunk to my bed. I felt meaner, and lowlier and more despicable than the worms. During all this time I had but one piece of money—a silver ten cent piece—and I held to it and would not spend it on any account, lest the consciousness coming strong upon me that I was entirely penniless, might suggest suicide. (*Roughing It*, Chapter 59)

Thoughts of suicide came often, and slinkings, as Sam referred to it, became a way of life to avoid meeting anyone he knew or owed money to. He saw himself as a miserable failure without any future and for weeks simply disappeared into San Francisco's back alleys and darkness to avoid the questioning eyes and commentary of those he knew.

Then, Sam's prospects changed when Steve Gillis got into a barroom brawl. Gillis was a small but powerfully built man who liked to fight just about as much as he liked to drink, and he and Clemens had many memorable drunken moments terrorizing the town together. Steve also had a violent temper, which exploded especially if he saw what he thought to be an injustice, just like the time when he passed by the saloon run by Big Jim Casey and found the barkeep pushing around a smaller patron whom Steve immediately defend-ed. Billy Gillis, Steve's brother, describes "The Fight That Made Mark Twain Famous" in his remembrances:

> When Steve interfered in the fight, Casey let the little man go, locked the door and put the key in his pocket. Then turning to Steve, he said, "Now Mister, as you have butted in without being asked, I'll fin-ish the job on you" and with these words he went at Steve with a rush. When Casey locked the door Steve stepped over to the bar and there stood waiting his onslaught; and when he got within striking distance, smashed him over the head with a big beer pitcher standing on the bar. This blow was a "down went Mc-Ginty" one for Casey, and he fell heavily to the floor, all the fight knocked out of him. (*Goldrush Days*, 53)

The "fight," such as it was, sent Casey, on the brink of death, to a local hospital, and Steve was immediately arrested on a charge of assault and battery, not knowing if Casey would live or die. Sam was told of Steve's arrest and had to find a way to free his friend so, pen-niless, he posted a $500 bond to secure his release from jail.

The next morning as they were on their way to the *Call* where Steve worked, they were informed by a police officer that Casey's head was terribly cut, he was delirious, and might well die. Steve knew that if Casey died, there were no witnesses to the fight and he might well be found guilty of killing Casey. Sam knew Steve had to skedaddle for his own safety, but Sam was in trouble, too. If Steve left and failed to appear in court, Sam would be required to post the $500 bail, which he didn't have, and he would go to jail. Billy Gillis retells what Steve told Sam in his own words:

SLINKING.

Illustration from Mark Twain's *Roughing It*

"Say, Sam," said Steve, "If I have to go back to Virginia City, and I guess I had better, you go up to my two brothers on Jackass Hill and stay with them until this thing blows over. They will be delighted to have you with them. It will be a splendid vacation and outing for you, and you will have the time of your life. It won't interfere in your engagements with the papers for which you are writing here, and you will be able to pick up a lot of things that will help you as a writer." (*Goldrush Days*, 58)

And so they went their separate ways—Steve back to the *Enterprise*—and Sam to the Mother Lode. George Williams III describes some of the reasons why Clemens left San Francisco for Jackass Hill in his history, *Mark Twain and the Jumping Frog of Calaveras County*:

At the time Twain left San Francisco for Jackass Hill, he was nearly broke and needed a place to stay. Twain admitted that he was unable to pay his landlady for room and board. Even after he returned from Jackass Hill, he spent more than a year paying off his debts. Besides being broke, Twain was just plain tired . . . . After quitting the *Call*, his struggles to earn a living as a free-lance writer and his failure to earn enough to cover living expenses increased Sam's mental stress . . . . Broke, stressed-out and mentally tired, Twain needed a rest. Twain's decision to leave San Francisco is in line with his lifelong work pattern: intense work followed by long rests. (Williams, *Mark Twain and the Jumping Frog of Calaveras County*, 34)

THE MOTHER LODE INFLUENCE

Jim Gillis is seated next to the door of the Gillis cabin. Second from the left is John Meiser's father, Frederick, 17 years old, who worked at the Longfellow Mining Company. Photo courtesy of John Meiser and the Mark Twain Project— The Bancroft Library, University of California, Berkeley.

THE CABIN ON JACKASS HILL

Jim Gillis (34), Billy Gillis (23), and Dick Stoker (46) lived on Jackass Hill and worked as pocket miners on their remaining claims along the Mother Lode when Sam, now 29 years old, arrived that winter of 1864. George Williams III describes the cabin in *Mark Twain and the Jumping Frog of Calaveras County*:

> Gillis and Stoker's one room cabin was about twenty feet long and ten feet wide and built in a grove of live oak trees. The cabin actually belonged to Dick Stoker who built it in 1850. At the west end of the dirt floor cabin, there was a stone fireplace whose mantel Jim Gillis leaned against while telling his impromptu stories. Twain described Gillis and Stoker's cabin in 1864, "No planking on the floor; old bunks, pans,

traps all kinds—Byron, Shakespeare, Bacon, Dickens, & every kind of only first class Literature" (37).

In Billy Gillis' personal collection of stories, *Goldrush Days with Mark Twain*, there are many stories about his efforts to learn how to become a success-

Billy Gillis stands by replica of cabin. Photo Courtesy of the Mark Twain Project— The Bancroft Library, University of California, Berkeley

ful miner. One story in *Goldrush*, "Experience of a Pocket Miner," describes his journey, in May of 1863, to try his luck as a miner and join his brother Jim and Dick Stoker on Jackass Hill in Tuolumne County. He took a steamer to Stockton, then a six-horse coach for the next sixty-mile ride, and "arrived in Sonora at six o'clock that evening tired, hungry, and dirtier than ever before in my life." The next day, after purchasing a pick, shovel, crowbar, sledge hammer and gold pan, he accompanied his brother Jim on the trail to Jackass Hill to take up life as a pocket miner.

The next morning Jim showed him a big, bold vein of quartz which may, or may not, have held a fortune in gold. Jim taught him how to dig out the quartz and break it up with his sledge hammer into smaller pieces the size of walnuts. He was to put some broken pieces of quartz into his pan, wash them in the ditch, and, if he saw no color, throw them away and get more broken quartz. Billy retells his first day's experience as a miner in *Goldrush Days*:

> By noon I had pounded about half a ton of rock into bits and washed about a half dozen pans in the ditch, and all I had to show for my work was sore muscles, blistered hands and my fingers all cut with

small fragments of sharp quartz. When I reached the cabin covered with dirt and reeking with sweat, Dick greeted me with, "What luck?"

"If you call this luck," I answered, "I've had lots of it," showing him my blistered hands and bleeding fingers. Then I told him of my half day's strenuous labor. "You certainly have got your hands into a pretty bad fix by pounding and panning that quartz and I am afraid that you'll have a lot of trouble with them. Go over to the sink and wash the dirt out of the cuts and I will see what I can do to relieve the pain and neutralize the poison in them."

"Poison, why how can there be poison in them, Mr. Stoker, and if there is, where did it come from?"

"From the quartz, of course; there is more or less poison in all quartz, and a cut from it will sometimes cause a bad sore unless it is promptly attended to."

As Billy tells it, Dick Stoker bandaged Billy's sore and wounded fingers and then suggested he take the rest of the day off, but Billy was having none of that. He went back to digging quartz saying he'd strike a pocket and bring back at least a thousand by evening. And he almost did!

I pried out an extra large one and coming down on it with a mighty whack it came apart with a sort of whine and there it lay before me held together by strands of coarse gold . . . . Well, I just dropped my hammer and shouldering the big boulder, started the five mile clip to the cabin . . . . When Dick's eyes caught the gleam of yellow metal his excitement nearly equaled my own . . . . My "cleanup" from this one rock amounted to a little over seven hundred dollars.

There are all manner of ways to calculate the value of a dollar from 1863 to today, but his $700 meant that Billy had just uncovered at least $20,000 in today's gold values. One rock equals one small fortune. But his luck wouldn't hold. Billy says, "I picked and shoveled, broke rock and panned, for three months after this 'lucky strike,' but my 'hunches' all went back on me and my eyes were never again gladdened by seeing another color of gold."

December found Billy Gillis back prospecting on Jackass Hill after months of finding nothing, but his luck would change again on January 8:

> On that day we found a prospect that developed into a pocket from which, in the next three days, we panned out seven thousand dollars. The gold from this pocket relieved us from all financial trouble and made me regard the world a pretty good old world after all. From this time until August, 1867, when I left Tuolumne County for Virginia City, I continued to prospect for quartz pockets with varying success, sometimes sailing before a fair wind over a sea of prosperity, at others wallowing, rudderless, among the breakers of adversity. (*Goldrush Days*)

Mark Twain would find Tuttletown almost deserted when he arrived, but Billy was there in its heyday as Billy relates:

> At this time Tuttletown was one of the liveliest towns in the county, mining both quartz and placer, being prospected vigorously with paying results to the miners . . . and an air of prosperity hung over all. There was one store, carrying a full stock of mer-

chandise such as groceries, boots and shoes, clothing and mining supplies; a hotel and barber shop and, of course, a saloon, where wine and whiskey were dispensed to the thirsty populace. Besides these business houses, there was a Literary Society, with a membership of three hundred, having a library of near a thousand volumes of standard prose and poetical works. (*Goldrush Days*, "Experience of a Pocket Miner")

But, good luck couldn't last. Like all placer mining in the Mother Lode, the gold would run out after several years of frantic digging. The creeks and streams would be stripped to bedrock, the tailings simply left in huge piles on the riverbanks. Coyote holes were dug wherever there was a likely quartz vein that might bring riches, but most of the digs did not. Miners, as Billy did in 1867, would leave worn out gold fields and find someplace else to go and any other life to live but that of a miner.

Swerner's Store, Tuttletown—Photo Courtesy of Tuolumne Historical Society

Sam Clemens arrived on Jackass Hill on December 4, 1864, a desperate man with thoughts of suicide. He would stay for 88 days and always recall that hillside as being, "that serene and reposeful and dreamy and delicious sylvan paradise" (*Autobiography*, Chapter 27).

The hill was barren and the remnants of a once-thriving community of Tuttletown, two miles away, could count only the Tuttletown Hotel, Swerner's Store, and a saloon. Sam could now find "half a dozen scattered dwellings were still inhabited and there was one saloon of a ruined and rickety character struggling for life, but doomed." This cabin was where their lives had come to a stop, and they had neither the energy nor inclination to move on. They subsisted by pocket mining—a tedious, laborious, and usually unsuccessful way to find small pockets of gold, a travail at which Clemens never succeeded (*Autobiography*, Chapter 26).

THE OLD COLLEGIATE.

Illustration from Mark Twain's
Roughing It

Twain would later describe the nature of life for a pocket miner on the hill in *Roughing It*:

> There are not now more than twenty pocket miners in that entire little region, and I think I know every one of them personally. I have known one of them to hunt patiently about the hillside every day for eight months without finding gold enough to make a snuffbox—his grocery bill running up relentlessly all the time—and then find a pocket and take out of it two thousand

dollars in two dips of his shovel. I have known him to take out three thousand dollars in two hours, and go and pay up every cent of his indebtedness, then enter on a dazzling spree that finished the last of his treasure before the night was gone. And the next day he bought his groceries on credit as usual, and shouldered his pan and shovel and went off to the hills hunting pockets again happy and content. This is the most fascinating of all the different kinds of mining, and furnishes a very handsome percentage of victims to the lunatic asylum. (*Roughing It*, Chapter 60)

STRIKING A POCKET.

Illustration from Mark Twain's *Roughing It*

Twain would include Jim Gillis and Dick Stoker stories in *Roughing It*. In Chapter 60, "An Old Friend," he describes meeting a friendly miner, the old collegiate, and pocket mining, the process they used for finding any remaining gold. In Chapter 61 he relates the tale of "Dick Baker and His Cat," the story of Tom Quartz, the cat who survived a disastrous mining experience with dynamite. Dick Baker was actually Dick Stoker, a man Twain would describe as "one of the gentlest spirits that ever bore its patient cross in a weary exile . . . . gray as a rat, earnest, thoughtful, slenderly educated, slouchily dressed and clay-soiled, but his heart was finer metal than any gold his shovel ever brought to light—than any, indeed, that ever was mined or minted" (*Roughing It*, Chapter 61).

Jim Gillis, Twain recalls, was a genius, extraordinarily well read, a great humorist with quick wit, affable, one of the greatest storytellers he ever heard, and excellent company, pretty much the definition of a Bohemian. For Clemens, the cabin and its keepers were comfortable, safe, invigorating, and the mantel held the best classical literature to be read; it was a wonderful place to enjoy the company of men who would become his true friends, men he respected and admired. In this cabin and company, Sam was happy and content while he skedaddled once again from his troubles and travails in the real world (*Autobiography*, Chapter 27).

Sam Clemens', and now Mark Twain's, life would be rejuvenated by the stay on the hill, a very special place with extraordinary men whose impact spread far beyond that little hill. When he heard of Jim Gillis' passing away in May, 1907, Twain wrote a long and thoughtful remembrance of the man he respected and whose memory he cherished:

Jim Gillis, Photo courtesy of Bank of Stockton Archives

I think Jim Gillis was a much more remarkable person than his family and his intimates ever suspected. He had a bright and smart imagination and it was the kind that turns out impromptu work and does it well, does it with easy facility and without previous preparation, just builds a story as it goes along, careless of whither it is proceeding, enjoying each fresh fancy as it flashes from the brain and caring not at all whether the story shall ever end brilliantly and satisfactorily or shan't end at all . . . . A genius is not very likely to ever discover himself; neither is he very likely to be discovered by his intimates . . . .

Every now and then Jim would have an inspiration and he would stand up before the great log fire, with his back to it and his hands crossed behind him and deliver himself of an elaborate impromptu lie—a fairy tale, an extravagant romance—with Dick Stoker as the hero of it as a general thing. Jim always soberly pretended that what he was relating was strictly history, veracious history, not romance. Dick Stoker, grey headed and good natured, would sit smoking his pipe and listen with a gentle serenity to these monstrous fabrications and never utter a protest.

I mourn for Jim. He was a good and steadfast friend, a manly one, a generous one; an honest and honorable man and endowed with a lovable nature. He instituted no quarrels himself but whenever a quarrel was put upon him he was on deck and ready. (*Autobiography*, Chapter 27)

SAM CLEMENS BEGINS A NEW NOTEBOOK

There is a four-year break in the notebooks written by Sam Clemens from July, 1861, the time he left the Mississippi as a pilot and the start of the Civil War, until January, 1865, New Year's Eve, when he pens his first notes in "Notebook Four" at Vallecito, California, during the start of his stay in the Mother Lode. His notes on that night include a reference to Jim Townsend, with whom he had worked at the *Territorial Enterprise*: "New Year's night—dream of Jim Townsend." It was Townsend who had written a version of the jumping frog story while working for the *Sonora Herald* in 1853, which explains why that ancient legend was continuing to be told in the foothills by folks like Ben Coon in Angels Camp, even though he couldn't tell it very well. (Williams, *Jumping Frog*, 54)

In January, Sam would write in "Notebook Four": "The Tragedian & Burning Shame. No women admitted." Clemens always thought the "Tragedian" done by Gillis and Stoker in front of the cabin fireplace was one of the most hilarious and wonderfully funny performances he'd ever seen. Jim Gillis told his stories with slow, fanciful descriptions, stopping to pause while the listener built visions and vistas in his own mind's eye—deadpan serious without ever cracking so much as a smile, the story told as absolute truth, in a matter-of-fact way. The evening was for men only, and Twain would have to wait until 1885 to include it in a book, but he lamented the revisions he had to make:

> In one of my books—Huckleberry Finn, I think—
> I have used one of Jim's impromptu tales, which I
> called "The Tragedy of the Burning Shame." I had
> to modify it considerable to make it proper for print
> and this was a great damage. As Jim told it, inventing it as it went along, I think it was one of the most
> outrageously funny things I have ever listened to.

How mild it is in the book and how pale; how extravagant and how gorgeous in the unprinted form! (*Autobiography*, Chapter 27)

Robinson's Ferry, on the Stanislaus River, which connected Jackass Hill to Angels Camp, near Vallecito.
Photo courtesy of the Calaveras County Historical Society

Gillis and Stoker had claims in the Angels Camp area across the river from Jackass Hill, and Sam went with Jim Gillis to stay in Angels in January to work the claims. The weather, however, was not agreeable; in fact, it was miserable with rain and cold, and the situation was made even worse by the wretched food prepared by the Frenchman. From "Notebook Four":

Jan. 23, 1865 – Angels – Rainy, stormy – Beans and dishwater/or breakfast at the Frenchman's, dishwater & beans for dinner, & both articles warmed over for supper.

24th – Rained all day – meals as before

25th – Same as above.

26th – Rain, beans & dishwater – tapidaro [leather cover from a Mexican stirrup] beefsteak for a change – no use, could not bite it.

27th – Same old diet – same old weather – went out to the "pocket" claim – had to rush back.

28th – Rain & wind all day & all night. Chili beans & dishwater three times to-day, as usual, & some kind of "slum" which the Frenchman called "hash." Hash be d—d.

29th – The old, old thing. We shall have to stand the weather, but as J [Jim] says, we won't have to stand this dishwater & beans any longer, by G—.

30th Jan. – Moved to the new hotel, just opened – food fare, & coffee that a Christian may drink without jeopardizing his eternal soul.

Feb. 3 – Dined at the Frenchman's in order to let Dick see how he [Frenchman] does things. Had Hellfire soup & the old regular beans & dishwater. The Frenchman has 4 kinds of soup which he furnishes to customers only on great occasions. They are popularly known among the borders as Hellfire, General Debility, Insanity & Sudden Death, but it is not possible to describe them. (Williams, *Mark Twain and the Jumping Frog of Calaveras County*, 56-57)

Finally, in February, the weather turned hot and the rain ceased. They would prospect the area around Angels, and Sam would "superintend" as usual, avoiding any kind of physical labor or exertion. He would fill his notebook with line after line about stories, people, events, and characters he heard about or encountered. After many unsuccessful days of hunting for gold but wonderful times spent together on the hillsides, they returned to Angels Camp. Sam had

*Angels Camp Hotel where Ben Coon told the Frog Story to Sam Clemens
Photo Courtesy of Calaveras County Historical Society*

written an earlier entry in his notebook that he, "met Ben Coon, Ill [Illinois], river pilot here" who was then a bartender at the Angels Camp Hotel. It was Ben Coon who would retell the frog story, and Sam would pen this note about the tale in his notebook:

> Coleman with his jumping frog—bet stranger $50— stranger had no frog, & C [Coleman] got him one— in the meantime stranger filled C's frog full of shot [lead pellets] & he couldn't jump—the stranger's frog won. (Williams, *Mark Twain and the Jumping Frog of Calaveras County*, 59)

Twain would later describe Ben Coon as being:

> . . . a dull person, and ignorant; he had no gift as a story-teller, and no invention; in his mouth this episode was merely history—history and statistics; and the gravest sort of history, too, he was entirely serious, for he was dealing with what to him were austere facts, and they interested him solely because they were facts; he was drawing on his memory, not his mind; he saw no humor in his tale, neither did his listeners; neither he nor they ever smiled or laughed . . . . (qtd. in Williams, *Mark Twain and the Jumping Frog of Calaveras County*, 60).

For Sam, Jim Gillis could tell a story, but Ben Coon could not.

Much later, and just before he married Olivia Langdon, Mark Twain wrote a letter to Jim Gillis about their hearing and retelling the frog story:

> You remember the one gleam of jollity, that shot across our dismal sojourn in the rain and mud of Angels Camp—I mean that day we sat around the tavern stove and heard that chap tell about the frog and how they filled him with shot. And you remember how we

quoted from the yarn and laughed over it, out there on the hillside while you and dear old Stoker panned and washed. I jotted down the story in my notebook that day and I would have been glad to get ten or fifteen dollars for it—I was just that blind. I published that story, and it became widely known in America, India, China, England—and the reputation it made for me has paid me thousands and thousands of dollars since . . . . wouldn't I love to take old Stoker by the hand and wouldn't I love to see him in his great speciality, his wonderful rendition of "Rinaldo" in the "Burning Shame!" Where is Dick and what is he doing? Give him my fervent love and warm old remembrances. (qtd. in Williams, *Mark Twain and the Jumping Frog of Calaveras County*, 75)

Sam would spend but three months on Jackass Hill before returning to San Francisco, but these months were life changing for the young writer. He lived with Jim Gillis, perhaps the greatest storyteller he ever heard, a man he deeply admired and respected. In *Mark Twain and the Jumping Frog of Calaveras County*, George Williams III writes about this very special relationship and bond between these two men:

Though Mark Twain lived with Jim Gillis a mere three months, for more than four decades afterward, Twain remembers Jim Gillis with love. Perhaps this was because Jim was part of the free living, adventurous years of Nevada and California that Mark Twain fondly recalled when old. More importantly, Jim Gillis was the leading character in Twain's stay in the California Gold Country which led to the discovery of the "Jumping Frog" story, the publication of which launched Twain's international career and eventually earned him thousands of dollars." (42)

For the first time since leaving the Mississippi, Sam would start writing in "Notebook Number Four", and fill it with all manner of observations, story lines, characters, incidents, and information. Some of these notes would find their way into his stories years later, with Tom Quartz the cat, a blue jay and acorns, the tragedian, and, of course, Ben Coon telling a story about a frog that couldn't jump. Many of these memories would feed his literary art for the rest of his life.

The Occidental Hotel, 1860, San Francisco. Photo courtesy of the Mark Twain Project—The Bancroft Library, University of California, Berkeley

BACK TO SAN FRANCISCO

Thoroughly refreshed and rejuvenated by his stay on Jackass Hill in the company of men he trusted and admired for their genius, good nature, and Bohemian ways, Sam left for San Francisco, arriving at the Occidental Hotel on February 26, 1865. With his new notebook filled with wonderful characters and stories, he took up writing again. He worked for the *Californian* and *Enterprise* and Mark Twain was steadily gaining a reputation as an exceptional humorist. Some of his articles were reprinted in Eastern newspapers, and the *New York Round Table* noted in October, 1865, that Twain was a rising star:

> The foremost among the merry gentlemen of the California press, as far as we have been able to judge, is one who signs himself "Mark Twain" . . . Perhaps, if he will husband his resources and not kill with overwork the mental goose that has given us these golden eggs, he may one day take rank among the brightest of our wits. (qtd. in Williams, *Mark Twain and the Jumping Frog of Calaveras County*, 69)

Upon returning to the Occidental Hotel, Sam had three months of mail waiting for him, including a letter from Artemus Ward reminding him to send a story for publication in the book he was writing about his Western adventures. Ward was an important man, a famous man, one essential to Clemens' future as a writer and performer, and Sam suggested the frog story. Ward said send it along. But Sam couldn't get the frog story right. In October, months too late to make the deadline, Clemens still hadn't settled on the story to submit and . . .

> Then one dismal afternoon as I lay on my hotel bed, completely nonplussed and about determined to

inform Artemus that I had nothing appropriate for his collection, a still small voice began to make itself heard.

Try me! Try Me! Oh, please try me! Please do!

It was the poor little jumping frog . . . that old Ben Coon had described! Because of the insistence of its pleading and for want of a better subject, I immediately got up and wrote out the tale for my friend who had followed up his first letter with several more requests. But if it hadn't been for that little fellow's apparition in this strange fashion, I never would have written about him—at least not at that time (Branch et al. *Early Tales & Sketches*, Volume 2, 266).

Clemens wrote the Jumping Frog story and sent it back East with the pen name Mark Twain, and it arrived as Ward's book was being printed. Ward's publisher, George Carlton, forwarded it to Henry Clap, editor of the New York Literary Newspaper, *Saturday Press*, without Twain's knowledge, and thus "Jim Smiley and His Jumping Frog" was published in the November 18, 1865, edition. From there, it was picked up by several newspapers, as was common practice at the time, and it went around the country and into history (Paine, Chapter 51).

Paine relates, "It brought the name of Mark Twain across the mountains, bore it up and down the Atlantic coast, and out over the prairies of the Middle West. Away from the Pacific slope only a reader here and there had known the name before. Now everyone who took a newspaper was treated to the tale of the wonderful Calaveras frog, and received a mental impression of the author's signature. The name Mark Twain hardly became an institution, as yet, but it made a strong bid for national acceptance" (Paine, Chapter 51).

In March, 1866, Sam sailed to the Sandwich Islands (Hawaii) as a correspondent for the *Sacramento Union* to describe the islands and all their delights and mysteries for Western readers and would send 25 letters back home with his vivid descriptions of life in that tranquil paradise. He returned in July, thoroughly broke and in desperate need of money once again. The idea of a public lecture about the islands, in the style of Artemis Ward, came to mind, and, using all his remaining funds he rented the largest hall in town, Maguire's Academy of Music in San Francisco, which seated 2,000 souls, for the night of October 2. Twain spent $150 on hand bills, which included one line that has become part of American folklore: "Doors open at 7½. The trouble will begin at 8" (*Roughing It*, Chapter 78).

Maguire's Academy of Music, San Francisco
Photo Courtesy of the Mark Twain Project—
The Bancroft Library, University of California, Berkeley

Sam was taking one of the greatest risks of his life, for his reputation would be ruined in so many ways if he were a failure at what he was about to attempt. In Chapter 78 of *Roughing It*, Twain describes his planning, preparation, and growing sense of doom and despair about the performance. Using words like tortured, break down, disconsolate, audacity, suspense dragged, grieved, panic-stricken, failure, suffered thought of suicide, gave myself up to the horrors, hadn't eaten in three days, face the horror, doomed to hang, he attempts to convey the terror he was going through, a terror many of us share if we even think about speaking before a group of people, and his was 2,000 strong. He walked onto the stage at eight, "staring at a sea of faces, bewildered by the fierce glare of the lights, and quaking in every limb with a terror that seemed like to take my life away. The house was full, aisles and all!" It was more than a minute before he calmed himself, and then he began to speak.

SEVERE CASE OF STAGE-FRIGHT.

Illustration from Mark Twain's
Roughing It

Paine describes how the lecture began:

> Expecting to find the house empty, he found it packed from the footlights to the walls. Sidling out from the wings—wobbly-kneed and dry of tongue— he was greeted by a murmur, a roar, a very crash of applause that frightened away his remaining vestig-

es of courage. Then, came reaction—these were his friends, and he began to talk to them. Fear melted away, and as tide after tide of applause rose and billowed and came breaking at his feet, he knew something of the exaltation of Monte Cristo when he declared "The world is mine! "(Paine, Chapter 54)

Mark Twain ends Chapter 78 of *Roughing It* with this comment about the performance: "All the papers were kind in the morning; my appetite returned; I had abundance of money. All's well that ends well." He delivered more than 20 lectures around the West and then, on December 15, 1866, boarded a ship for New York City. The "Jumping Frog" story had made him famous as a humorous writer, and his lectures would make him one of the world's most famous stage performers.

LEAVING CALIFORNIA FOR NEW YORK

After reaching New York, Twain decided to become a fellow passenger and correspondent on the very first tourist excursion to Europe and the Holy Land. The *Quaker City* was chartered and plans were prepared for the first American visitors to take this kind of voyage of discovery. Upon his return he wrote *Innocents Abroad*, or *The New Pilgrims' Progress*, (1869), which would become his best-selling work ever, and planned a lecture tour across America including some of his old favorite haunts in California and Nevada.

Billy Gillis, by this time a reporter for the *Enterprise* in Virginia City just as Sam Clemens had been, saw the second of two performances by Twain scheduled for Piper's Opera House, April 27 and 28, 1868. He describes Twain's performance in his book, *Memories of Mark Twain and Steve Gillis:*

> His person, his pose, his manner of delivery and his drawling voice, were so perfectly in accord with

his subject matter that from the first word to the last, the interest of his audience never for a moment flagged. He would at times have the people in tears by telling them stories of suffering in the Holy City; of little children starving in the streets; of decrepit old men and women sitting by the wayside with shriveled arms and hands held out for alms; and of the lame, the halt and the blind, huddled together to warm their diseased and almost naked bodies.

He would then throw them into convulsions of laughter with one of his ludicrous stories, all the while looking as serious as an owl.

. . . When Sam ended his lecture . . . his audience went wild, and he stood bowing and smiling for full ten minutes before the cheering and other demonstrations of appreciation ended . . . . His tour came to an end with his lecture at Carson. From here he returned to Virginia City and after bidding his friends goodbye, left the state.

I never met Sam after this parting, but the personality of this wonderful man is indelibly stamped upon my memory and he stands just as clearly before me today as in the years of Long Ago, when we were both young men in the hey-day of our lives.

Ah well! so we move on. We are here today and "over there" tomorrow and then—who knows. (Gillis, *Memories* 92-94)

Billy wants us to remember how Mark Twain's life was forever altered by a barroom brawl in San Francisco when he was without hope and thinking about suicide:

Opportunity knocked at his door when Steve had his famous fight with Big Jim Casey. Had that fight not occurred, he would not have gone to Jackass Hill. Had he not gone to Jackass Hill the "Jumping Frog" and "Roughing It" would not have been written. No letters from the Islands would have made the world laugh and the story of "Innocents Abroad" would not have been told. Consequently we must conclude that Mark Twain owed his quick transition from a newspaper correspondent to the greatest humorist of his time to that mixup between Steve and Casey on that day in September, 1864 (*Goldrush Days with Mark Twain*, 60).

None of the Gillis clan would ever see Sam Clemens again, and their adventures together in the West, and on Jackass Hill, came to a close.

When Sam Clemens arrived at Jackass Hill in December, 1864, he was penniless, dispirited, and had thoughts about committing suicide. The cabin would be his refuge, a safe haven, a place he would later call, "that serene and reposeful and dreamy and delicious sylvan paradise." He stayed with Jim Gillis, Billy Gillis, and Dick Stoker, surviving by pocket mining, a laborious and seldom successful process for finding the remaining gold.

The cabin was the center of Bohemian culture in the Mother Lode, with the best literature on the mantel, and it was frequented by writers like Bret Harte who wanted to spend time with its most congenial, brilliant host, Jim Gillis. On New Year's Eve, Sam Clemens started his first notebook since leaving the Mississippi River—"Number Four" at Vallecito. Sam decided he had a future as a writer, and the new notebook would provide new material.

At the Angels Camp Hotel, he heard Ben Coon tell a tale about a frog filled with buckshot and Twain would write a famous note about a frog who couldn't jump.

Returning to San Francisco refreshed and ready to start over, Twain slowly built up a successful writing career and paid off his debts, but he owed Artemus Ward a story. It was months later, in October, 1865, when he wrote "Jim Smiley and His Jumping Frog," and sent it back East with the pen name of Mark Twain. After years of writing for the *Enterprise*, *Californian*, and other papers and journals, he would take that one note about the frog and turn it into a complete, masterful story with characters and descriptions drawn from those he had seen in years past, using Western dialects and conversations. For readers, it was as if they were there, listening to the people talk. It was the language of the West—rough, uncultured, filled with local color—and few other American writers have ever done it so well. That voice would be heard live, as well as in print, when he would make a name for himself as a lecturer, taking his humor to the stage.

The *Sacramento Union* hired him to travel to the Sandwich Islands and write descriptions of what he saw because they knew he could do it so well. Upon his return to San Francisco, those descriptions would become the material for a lecture given at Maguire's Music Hall, his first public performance. Artemus Ward was the model for his stage performance, and Jim Gillis was the source of how he told his stories. Twain was a resounding success and would be one of the world's most famous speakers and successful stage performers for the next 30-plus years.

It was a far cry from an earlier stage in his career, when an almost hopeless Sam Clemens arrived on Jackass Hill on December 4, 1864. Just two years later, a soon-to-be world-famous Mark Twain left California for New York. Certainly all things good that were to happen to Sam Clemens and Mark Twain don't begin and they don't end with his 88 days in the Mother Lode, but it is interesting to speculate about what would have happened to Sam Clemens if Steve Gillis hadn't gotten into a barroom fight and broken that beer pitcher over Big Jim Casey's head.

Thoughtful reflections of Mark Twain ~

"No man is a failure who has friends."

"Whoever is happy will make others happy too."

"Get your facts first and then you can distort them as much as you please."

BILLY GILLIS AND HIS MEMORIES OF MARK TWAIN

❝ *But the personality of this wonderful man is indelibly stamped upon my memory and he stands just as clearly before me today as in the years of Long Ago, when we were both young men in the hey-day of our lives.* **❞**

~ William R. Gillis

William R. (Billy) Gillis was the brother of Steve and Jim Gillis and lived on Jackass Hill with brother Jim and Dick Stoker when Sam Clemens arrived in December, 1863. He wrote a collection of memories of those days, *Goldrush Days with Mark Twain*, published by Albert & Charles Boni in 1930, which has 35 stories. The first story in the Goldrush book, "Experience of a Pocket Miner," is a narrative of how he learned to become a pocket miner on Jackass Hill, and parts of that story were included in this retelling of what life was like on Jackass Hill.

A second edition of this book, *Memories of Mark Twain and Steve Gillis*, published by *The Banner* in Sonora, California, included 24 of the original 35 Gillis stories along with this dedication by Billy:

DEDICATION

To the memory of my old friend, Dick Stoker, who, for so many years, lived with me in the "Mark Twain Cabin" on Jackass Hill, this book is lovingly dedicated. Dear old Dick! He belonged to no religious sect nor creed, but his heart overflowed with love for his fellowmen, and by his obedience to the Great Commandment,

"Thou Shalt Love Thy Neighbor As Thyself," he has proven title to a home in the "Beautiful Isle of Somewhere."

And, on the same page, Billy penned a word about the stories he was about to tell:

JUST A WORD

In the story contained in this book, I have made no attempt at flowery writing, nor have I endeavored to paint any glowing word pictures that would have a tendency to place it among the classics. It is just a plain story of people and happenings of long ago, told in plain words.

Many of the occurrences recorded in these pages were both tragic and dramatic, while in some of them my readers may find something they may deem humorous enough to cause a smile.

The story is essentially true in every detail, and I am confident that it will receive a fair measure of appreciation by all those interested in stories of the past.

~ W.R.GILLIS

BILLY GILLIS &

HIS GOLD RUSH STORIES

With MARK TWAIN

Seven of Billy's stories follow—those most directly involving Sam Clemens himself. They provide wonderful insights into the eccentric and sometimes hostile nature of Sam Clemens' character, beloved by his cabin mates, but possessing a volcanic temper, reacting with furious responses to having any jokes or pranks played on him, with his adamant refusal to do any kind of normally expected work or labor.

ENTER SAMUEL CLEMENS

In 1861 Joe Goodman and Dagget McCarthy established the *Territorial Enterprise* at Virginia City. Steve, my brother, was foreman of the composing room.

Mark Twain had been writing news items for the *Enterprise* for something like a year when Goodman offered him a place as reporter on the paper. One night, shortly after this offer had been made, while Joe and Dagget were sitting in the editorial room enjoying a quiet smoke waiting for "copy" from the composing room a young man with a great bushy shock of brown hair entered, and a long-drawling voice said, "Does either of you gentlemen happen to be Mr. J. T. Goodman?"

"I am Joe Goodman," said Joe. "Can I do anything for you?"

"Mr. Goodman, if you will just look me over I think you will observe that the clothes I have on would not be suitable ones to wear at a fashionable tea party, also that a hair-cut and a shave, together with a new hat, would greatly improve my personal appearance. A bath, too, would feel mighty good to me, and a steak or a dish of ham and eggs would be very satisfying."

"My friend," said Joe, with a broad smile. "If you will just look this room over, I think you will observe that it is neither a clothing store, nor a barber shop. You will find, also, that there is no cuisine connected with it. I am sorry for you, but you have come to the wrong place, and will have to apply elsewhere."

The stranger, presenting a letter, said, "Mr. Goodman, if you will read this letter, I think you will agree with me that my reception has not been as cordial as I was led to expect it would be."

"Well, by the Great Hornspoon," exclaimed Joe, dropping the letter, "Dagget, this is Sam Clemens, and I'll be darned if he hasn't put one over on us this time, all right. Why didn't you say who you were in the first place, Sam, instead of beating around the bush in the way you did? But never mind, we're mighty glad you are here. Sit down. Dagget, step to the window and tell Steve to come here."

Dagget went to the window connecting the editorial and composing rooms and at the top of his voice shouted, "Steve Gillis! You are wanted in the editorial room." Steve lost no time in answering this summons, but came on the run. On entering, he saw Joe sitting at the table with Dagget standing just behind him, while on the opposite side stood an unshaven, roughly clad individual shaking his bushy head, and, as Steve thought, frowning at Joe. Appearances seemed to call for action, and Steve began to roll up his sleeves.

"There is no trouble, Steve. I just called you in to make you acquainted with Sam Clemens. Mr. Clemens this is our foreman, Steve Gillis."

With one of his hearty laughs, Steve started, with extended hand, across the room, saying, "Why, Mr. Clemens, I am surely glad to see you, although you don't look a bit like the Sam Clemens pictured in my mind."

"Mr. Gillis," said Sam. "I don't often cotton to a man on first acquaintance, but I do cotton to you, right here and now, and I know that we're going to be friends right from the start."

And so it proved to be. There was never a truer or closer friendship between two people than that between Sam and Steve.

"Steve," said Joe, "Sam has walked all the way from Aurora here and thinks he needs some repairs. You go down to the office with him and tell Charlie Bicknell to let him have the money he needs, and then get Mike's boy to pilot him to the places he wishes to patronize.

"Mike's boy, nothing," said Steve. "Just wait till I put Joe Harlow in charge of the forms, and I'll go myself."

After Sam had provided himself with a suit of clothes, had a haircut, shave and a bath, he and Steve went to the "White House" where they had a hearty supper. Then they returned to the office, where Sam kept them until morning telling, in his droll way, of his experiences from Aurora to Virginia City.

The morning after his arrival Clemens took charge of the local columns of the *Enterprise*. Associated with him was Dan De Quille, another writer widely known all over the coast as a humorist of exceptional ability. These two men kept the people along the Comstock continually laughing.

In December, 1862, Steve went from Virginia City to San Francisco and took a case on the *Morning Call*. Here he continued to work until September, 1864. After Steve left, Sam became low-spirited and did not seem at all like himself. He had lost his friend and could not be comforted. He stood his loneliness for two weeks and then resigned his position and followed Steve to San Francisco, saying that he knew Steve would get into some kind of trouble, and it was his duty to get him out of it. This prophecy of Sam's was literally fulfilled later on.

Billy Gillis in the shade of the oak tree outside the cabin on Jackass Hill.
Photo Courtesy of the Mark Twain Project—The Bancroft Library,
University of California, Berkeley

THE FIGHT THAT MADE MARK TWAIN FAMOUS

One night when on his way home from work, in passing the saloon of "Big Jim" Casey, on Howard Street, Steve saw a big ruffian unmercifully beating a little chap who had no more show with Casey than a rat would have with a terrier. Now, Steve was ever ready to help the weak against the strong, and the spectacle he was witnessing irresistibly called upon him to hasten to the relief of the little fellow in distress. So, without hesitation, he entered the saloon and took part in the fray. When Steve interfered in the fight, Casey let the little man go, locked the door and put the key in his pocket. Then turning to Steve, he said, "Now Mister, as you have butted in without being asked, I'll finish the job on you." And with these words he went at Steve with a rush.

When Casey locked the door Steve stepped over to the bar and there stood waiting his onslaught; and when he got within striking distance, smashed him over the head with a big beer pitcher standing on the bar. This blow was a "down went McGinty" one for Casey, and he fell heavily to the floor, all the fight knocked out of him.

Now was the time for Steve to make his get-away, but the key of the door being in Casey's pocket, he had no way of leaving the saloon, so he quietly stood and waited until Billy Blitz and another officer appeared upon the scene. Blitz at once stooped to examine Casey. Finding him unconscious, with blood streaming from his scalp, he summoned an ambulance and had him conveyed to the county hospital. He then arrested Steve and took him to the police station, where a charge of assault and battery was preferred against him.

Mark Twain, being summoned, went on Steve's bond in the sum of five hundred dollars, and he was released. When the two friends left the Hall of Justice they walked along in silence for a short distance, with Sam in the lead, shaking his head and muttering to himself. Sam's aloofness on this occasion was so unusual that Steve couldn't comprehend it, so at last he hailed him with, "Hold on, Sam, don't be in such a hurry. What's the matter with you, anyhow?"

"I'm mad, that's what's the matter, if you want to know, you confounded jackass. I am disgusted with you and don't care to have any talk with you at all."

"Why, Sam, I don't see that I have done anything so awful as to cause you to feel like that towards me."

"Oh, you don't, don't you? You didn't deliberately get into a mixup with Big Jim Casey over an affair that didn't concern you, did you? Why didn't you go on home last night, like a decent man? If you had, none of this trouble would have occurred. You would not now be booked at the city prison as a law breaker and a criminal and my name would not be registered there, as the friend and bondsman of a scrapping idiot. Instead of acting like a sensible person and attending to your own affairs, you had to go and jump into the dirty row. Oh! You have thrown the fat in the fire this time, young man."

"I say, Sam, you are going too far. You must let up on that kind of talk! I did no more than any man with the least humanity in his heart would have done in the same circumstances. When I got as far as Casey's saloon, on my way home, I saw the big man literally wiping up the floor with a little shrimp of a man, who was no more able to contend with him than a sparrow would be with a cat. He was just beating that poor little chap to a frazzle. Sam, I couldn't stand for anything like that, and I had to get in and stop Casey. I had no intention of getting into a fight with him. I only meant to make him let up on the little man and then go on home. When I interfered he quit beating the little fellow, but, instead of quieting down and behaving himself like a decent man, he locked the door and, putting the key in his pocket, came for me with head down, like a mad bull. I saw he intended to butt me in the stomach, so I grabbed the pitcher from the bar, and, when he got within reach, smashed him over the head with it. No, Sam, that is all there is to this assault and battery business. He is the one who made the assault and I, in self defense, stopped him with the pitcher."

"Yes, you stopped him all right, and I guess all that you have told me is true, but when this case comes to trial, if it ever does, what you have just told me is not going to help you, for the reason that you have no witness to substantiate your story."

"Well, Sam, here we are at the house. Let's stop talking about it till later on and, for goodness sake, don't let mother and the girls know anything about it."

"Haven't you got brains enough in that thick head of yours to know that a policeman couldn't come here at 2 o'clock in the morning and snake me off to the station house without them knowing that you were in trouble? You should have thought of your mother and sisters before you went into that rotten row. Steve Gillis, you make me sick. Come on and let's get to bed."

The next morning as they were on their way to the *Call* office they met Officer Blitz.

"Billy," said Sam, "have you heard anything of Casey's condition since this morning?" "Yes, I have, and it is a mighty serious one. His scalp is frightfully cut, and at 10 o'clock this morning he was raving in delirium. Steve, you hit Jim a hell of a lick with that pitcher, and I wouldn't wonder if he's knocked out for good. I am mighty sorry, Steve, but I am afraid you are going to have a heap of trouble getting out of this business."

After Blitz left them, Sam and Steve continued on their way. "Steve, from what Billy has just told us, it looks like Jim Casey has a good chance to die. If he does, you are going to have the devil's own time getting out of this rotten scrape. The only way I see that you can get out of it is to skip out of San Francisco and go back to your case on the *Enterprise*."

"And when you get out of here, what's going to happen to me, do you think?" asked Clemens. "When the case is called for trial and you fail to appear, your bonds will be declared forfeited. Dave Louderbach will then hail me to court and try to make me put up five hundred dollars for being fool enough to go on your bonds. I'll have to either pay the money or go to jail, and I don't want to do either."

"Say, Sam," said Steve, "If I have to go back to Virginia City, and I guess I had better, you go up to my two brothers on Jackass Hill and stay with them until this thing blows over. They will be delighted to have you with them. It will be a splendid vacation and outing for you, and you will have the time of your life. It won't interfere in your engagements with the papers for which you are writing here, and you will be able to pick up a lot of things that will help you as a writer."

MARK GOES TO JACKASS HILL

So it was arranged. Steve left the next day for Virginia City, where he resumed work as a compositor. A few days after Steve's departure Sam left for Jackass Hill, where he was the guest of myself and my brother Jim for something like months.

During the time of his visit to us, Sam Clemens never left Jackass Hill, except for a short time spent at Angels Camp, Calaveras County, when he gathered data for the "Jumping Frog of Calaveras" and "Roughing It". Steve became a prophet when he said to him, "You will be able to pick up lots of things that will help you as a writer." With the publication of these two books his career as the greatest humorist of his time really began.

Shortly after his return to San Francisco from his sojourn on the "Hill," Sam was sent with a party of United States surveyors to the Sandwich Islands as correspondent of the *Alta California*. While on this trip he wrote a series of letters for that paper which made the people laugh and cry all over the world. Returning to California, he lectured in all the principal cities of the coast on his experiences in the Islands and was enthusiastically received everywhere.

Shortly after completing his course of lectures on the Sandwich Islands he was sent by James Gordon Bennett of the *New York Herald* to the Holy Land as the special correspondent of the *Herald*. He accompanied a party of eminent divines, who went there on a voyage of discovery and research among the sacred places of Palestine. It was while on this journey that he collected the data for what a great many regard as his greatest work—"The Innocents Abroad." Coming back from the Holy Land he delivered another series of lectures on that historic country.

Mark Twain's fame was now assured and he was anchored in the hearts of the people of the whole world. Opportunity knocked at his door when Steve had his famous fight with Big Jim Casey. Had that fight not occurred, he would not have gone to Jackass Hill. Had he not gone to Jackass Hill the "Jumping Frog" and "Roughing It" would not have been written. No letters from the Islands would have made the world laugh and the story of "Innocents Abroad" would not have been told. Consequently we must conclude that Mark Twain owed his quick transition from a newspaper correspondent to the greatest humorist of his time to that mixup between Steve and Casey on that day in September, 1864.

In 1866 Steve was again made foreman of the composing room of the *Enterprise*, continuing as such until his marriage to Miss Kate Robinson, a niece of Mrs. J. T. Goodman, in December, 1867. After his marriage he took up his residence in San Francisco, working at the case there until 1871. In that year Goodman appointed him news editor of the *Enterprise*. This position he ably filled until the paper suspended publication in 1877.

He was then given the same position on the *Virginia City Chronicle,* owned by D. E. McCarthy, one of the founders of the *Enterprise*. He kept his place on the Chronicle until 1894, when he left Virginia City for the last time, going to Jackass Hill, Tuolumne County, where he engaged in quartz mining with his son, James A. Gillis.

Here he spent the remainder of his life, crossing the Great Divide into that Unknown Country which lies beyond the Dark Valley of Death on April 13, 1918. Steve was not a member of any Christian church, and for that reason was regarded by some professing Christians as a man living without religion in the world, but I, knowing him better, perhaps, than any living person, know that he was a Christian in the truest sense. The Bible was his constant companion, and he was more familiar with its sacred precepts and promises than the great majority of professing Christians. He was a firm believer in the Fatherhood of God and the brotherhood of man; broadminded and charitable; a friend to the friendless, and a helper in the time of need. I know that when his call came he did not go out into the darkness alone, but that the same kind hand that guided him through this vale of tears led him through the valley of shadow of death into the "New Jerusalem," where the wicked cease from troubling and the weary are at rest.

I have been visited by many people and questioned by them regarding Mark Twain's stay on Jackass Hill and his activities while there, and have listened to so many fictitious stories in connection therewith, that it will not tire my readers, perhaps, if I refute some of these stories and relate one or two happenings connected with Mark's visit.

I was interviewed on one occasion by a gentleman from the east who, after I told him all that I thought would interest him, asked, "Is that shaft still open where Mark came near losing his life by the explosion of a blast of dynamite because the man tending the hoist went to sleep?"

"That is a story," said I, "that I never heard. Tell me about it?" "Well, Mark had drilled a hole at the bottom of the shaft, loaded it with a heavy charge of dynamite, lighted the fuse and rang for the skip. After waiting several minutes without receiving any response to his signal, he rang again. The result was the same. By this time the fuse had burned pretty close to the top of the hole. Mark then concluded that further delay would be dangerous, so he took his knife from his pocket and quietly whetting it on his boot, cut the fuse when the fire was within half an inch of the mouth of the hole. Ringing the bell again, he sat calmly down, lit his pipe and patiently waited for his partner to hoist him to the surface. In about half an hour he heard a sound like someone stepping on the platform, and raising his voice, called, 'Oh, Dick!' "

"An answer came back, 'Hello, down there. Anything wanted?'" "Well, yes, if it is convenient I would like to be hoisted to the top.'"

"When the skip reached the bottom Mark rang three bells—meaning 'man aboard, go slow'— and, relighting the fuse, stepped into the skip and rang the signal to hoist. When he arrived at the surface, his partner said to him, 'Why didn't you ring the bell, Sam, instead of calling?' I did ring the bell, but it brought no results. Where have you been?"

"Nowhere. I've been right here all the time. Why do you ask?"

"Oh, I just wanted to know, that's all. But your failure to answer my signals to hoist came very near causing you to lose your partner, and me, my life. How did it happen that you failed to hear the bell?"

"Well, Sam, you know that it was nearly morning when I got home from the dance. I was feeling pretty rocky, and after I lowered you down the shaft I laid down with my coat for a pillow to take a little rest. I didn't intend to, but I must have gone to sleep."

"Now Dick, I don't want you to think for a moment that I have any hard feelings towards you, but your going to sleep on this occasion came very near causing my death, but I am as much alive as ever, so we'll just forget it and go to dinner."

If such an experience as the above could have possibly come to Sam Clemens, instead of talking the incident over with Dick in a calm and friendly way, he would probably have grabbed a drill, pick handle or any other weapon coming handy and brained him with it.

FUN ON THE HILL

Getting into Tuttletown at a rather late hour one night on my way home from Sonora, I found a party of half a dozen young men who had been serenading their lady friends in the neighborhood. I suggested that they go with me to Jackass Hill and end the night's program with a serenade to Mark Twain. They readily fell in with my suggestion and we climbed the hill together, and, after our chief musician had tuned up his "old banjo", lined up under Mark's window, and opened up with "Oh, Darkies, hab you seen Ole Massa?"

We had finished this song and "Happy Land O' Canaan" and were well under way with "I'se Gwine to de Shuckin," when that window went up with a bang, and an angry, rasping voice snarled out, "What do you lot of yapping coyotes mean by disturbing the peace and quiet of the respectable people on the hill with that infernal yowling you're doing out there? Get away from this window, you drunken loafers, and go off to that shuckin you're howling about, and go right now."

This rude reception, it is needless to say, put an abrupt ending to our serenade and my companions left the hill on the double quick. On entering the cabin I found Mark sitting on the side of the bed, cramming his pipe with "Bull Durham" tobacco. "Hello, Sam," said I, "going to have a smoke?"

At my salutation he looked at me with an ugly scowl and greeted me with, "Billy, how did you come to get drunk tonight, and bring that gang of low down rowdies on the hill, to make the night hideous with their horrible racket? Up to this time I have regarded you as a well-behaved, decent young fellow with instincts somewhat approaching those of a gentleman but I have been wakened from that dream to-night to find you nothing but a common, wine-guzzling hoodlum."

"Why, Sam," said I, "I am very sorry that you regard me in such a

light, and if you will think for a moment I believe that you will ad-
mit that you are doing me an injustice. I had no thought, nor did the
other boys, of giving offense by singing for you tonight. Our only intention or desire was to give you pleasure, for you know, Sam, that
upon the occasion of our visit to the young ladies of French Flat you
told me that 'music had charms to soothe the savage' and advised me
to cultivate—if I had any—my talent for it, and I was led to believe
from what you said that you loved music."

"Music! Great Scott, do you call that music? Why, the bleatings of
Carrington's band of goats are like strain of melody from the heav-
enly choir compared to that horrible caterwauling you were doing
there. Music, indeed, huh."

"Oh, well, Sam," said I, "I see now that I had the wrong coon up
a tree, and I ask your pardon. Come, shake hands, and be my friend
again, and I promise that there will be no repetition of tonight's
work."

"I'll have to do some serious thinking before I give you my friendship again, and as to shaking hands with you while in your present
maudlin condition, I tell you, Billy Gillis, I won't do it. Take off your
drunken debauch. Get over, as far as you can, to the other side of
the bed, and turn your face to the wall, for the fumes of that infernal
stuff you call wine that you have loaded up with, make me sick at my
stomach."

"All right, Sam. Good night."

Shortly after Sam returned to the "hill" from Angels Camp, the
boys instituted a "Hospital for the Insane" on Jackass Hill. Our of-
ficers consisted of a board of directors and a resident physician, the
rest of us constituting the attendants and patients. The "doctor" held
office for one week, then gave place to one of the others. When Sam's
turn came he sent in something like the following report:

"To the honorable board of directors of the Hospital for Insane on Jackass Hill.

Gentlemen: I have the honor to present to your honorable body the following report of my administration of the affairs of this institution for the week ending February—1865. I am happy to state that, with one exception, the inmates under my care are rapidly approaching complete recovery and I am greatly encouraged to believe that they will soon be in full possession of their mental faculties. The exception, noted above, is a young man named James N. Gillis. In all respects save one this patient's mind is in perfectly normal state. He is a very companionable young fellow, and tells some fairly humorous stories, and it is sad to know that this young man, who would otherwise be a useful member of society, is hopelessly insane, but such, I am sorry to say, is the truth. He is laboring under the hallucination that he is the greatest pocket miner on earth; that he can save more gold in panning out and appraising the value of a 'cleanup' before weighing; and the only miner having a perfect knowledge of gold-bearing ledges and formations. He is a fairly good pocket hunter and knows a gold nugget from a brass door knob, but there are a dozen of the boys on the hill who can give him cards and spades and beat him at the game."

This report of Sam's was received by the boys with a shout of merriment, Jim joining in the laugh at his own expense. The next week Jim was the doctor. His report to the "board of directors" read like this:

"One of the most pitiful cases of insanity that has ever fallen under my observation is that of a young man named Samuel L. Clemens, who was committed to this hospital on the thirteenth day of last month, from Angels Camp, Calaveras County. In my conversation with him on the day after he came under my care he seemed to be perfectly rational and in full possession of all his mental faculties. I was greatly encouraged to hope that after a short treatment to improve his physical and nervous condition he would be restored to his friends and society and again take his place as a useful worker in the affairs of the world. It was but a short time, however, when this hope was rudely shattered, and I found that he was hopelessly insane. He has, for the past three years, been associated with newspaper men of rare literary ability. He is obsessed with the idea that they are the spokes of the wheel and himself the hub around which they revolve. He has a mania for story writing, and is at the present time engaged in writing one entitled "The Jumping Frog of Calaveras," which he imagines will cause his name to be handed down to posterity from generation to generation as the greatest humorist of all time. This great story of his is nothing but a lot of silly drivel about a warty old toad that he was told of by some joker in Angels Camp. Every evening when the inmates are together in the living room, he takes up his manuscript and reads to them a page or two of the story and then winds up with, 'It's no wonder, that darned old frog couldn't jump worth shucks, boys, filled up with shot like he was.' Then he will chuckle to himself and murmur about 'copyrights' and 'royalties.' If this was the only trouble with Mark Twain, as he dubs himself in his stories, there would be a reasonable hope of the ultimate restoration of his mentality, but the one great hallucination that will forever bar him from the 'busy walks of life' is that he was at one time a pilot on one of the great Mississippi River packets which plied between St. Louis and New Orleans. He delights to tell of his experiences while navigating one of these big boats on the great river, of how his knowledge of its currents and bends, its shoals and eddies, and the dangerous snags along its banks, saved his boat and the lives of his passengers by his quick manipulation of the wheel. Poor Mark! His nearest approach to being a pilot on the river was when he handled the big steering paddle of a flat boat, freighted with apples from

Ohio, which were peddled in towns along the river."

This report of "Doctor" Jim was received by all the boys except Sam, with roars of laughter and applause, but nothing of the kind came from him. On the contrary, he sat through its reading livid with rage. After the merriment had somewhat subsided he opened on the boys with "You lot of laughing jackals! You think the rotten hogwash read to you by that empty-headed idiot, Jim Gillis, is mighty funny, don't you? I have had the impression up to tonight that you fellows had a few brains stowed away somewhere in your cocoanut heads, but I now see my mistake, and find that I have been associating with a crowd of ignorant, grinning apes, instead of intelligent human beings. I appreciate a joke, and love fun as much as anybody in the world, but when a lot of rotten stuff like Jim Gillis' funny hash is pulled off on me I am ready to cry quits. I do quit right now, and will have nothing more to do with your fool funny business."

Sam did like fun, but not when the fun was at his expense. There was never another meeting of the directors and inmates of the "hospital," Jim's report causing the institution to close for good. For a few days after this the boys kept Sam at fever heat with anger by asking him such questions as, "Say, Sam, how many barrels of apples could you load on to that flat-bottomed scow?" "Sam, how long did it take you to float that flatboat from St. Louis down to New Orleans?"

This chaffing so exasperated Sam that Jim requested the boys to stop it, fearing that he would leave the hill altogether. It was but a short time after this that he did leave and return to San Francisco, greatly to the regret of all the jolly good fellows whose esteem and friendship he had won while with them on the hill.

Just previous to his departure for Honolulu I received a letter from Sam, which ended as nearly as I can now remember, as follows:

"I am leaving San Francisco in a short time for the Sandwich

Islands in company with a party of U. S. surveyors, as special correspondent of the *Alta California*. As in the course of human events we
may not meet again, I will unburden my conscience of a load it has
been carrying ever since the night of the serenade you and your band
of troubadours attempted to give me. When you came into the cabin
after I had scared the other boys off the hill, I was in a mighty ugly
mood and I wanted just the chance you gave me to vent my spleen
on somebody or something. I called you some pretty hard names,
which I knew at the time were undeserved, and accused you of high
crimes and misdemeanors of which I knew you were not guilty. I
wanted to ask your pardon the next morning when you called me
to breakfast, but courage failed me and I put off doing so to a more
'convenient season.' That season has now arrived, and I do ask you
to forgive me. Tell the boys that I am often with them in my dreams,
and that when I return to the city I will come back to them once
more on Old Jackass, if I can possibly arrange to do so."

Sam never visited the hill again. After his return to California his
time was so fully occupied in preparation for his lecturing tour on
his trip to the Islands that he found it impossible to gratify his wish
to do so. It will be remarked that in this narrative I have but seldom
used his nom de plume of Mark Twain. He has always been to me,
and to all his other friends and companions who roughed it with
him in the days of yore, not the great humorist whose name is a
household word over the whole world, but just plain Sam—good old
Sam—one of the boys.

CLEMENS' ONE MINING VENTURE

The nearest approach to any work that Mark Twain ever did at mining was when he became my partner at one time for about two weeks. One day when on my way home from Sonora I took a short cut across a parcel of land from which the surface dirt had been washed by the placer miners some years before. While walking over this ground I came to a spot where the croppings of a reef of very fine mineral slate had been uncovered, and upon a closer examination, discovered a small quartz vein with a clay casing running through this body of slate. The chances for finding a "pocket" here looked mighty good to me, and I determined to return the next day and give it a try-out. Putting a piece of the quartz in my pocket, I continued on my way home. On entering the cabin I found Sam just sitting down to supper.

"Hello, Billy," said he, "you are just in time for the feast. I won't sing the praises of the bacon, but I'll bet your stomach never entertained flapjacks like these in your life."

After supper I handed him the quartz and said, "Sam, the chances for finding a pocket where I got that rock look mighty good to me. Go over with me in the morning and we'll go snooks in anything we find."

"All right, if you are willing to take me in, knowing that I know nothing about pocket mining, I will go in with you and we'll try and dig out a million or two."

Next morning, on arriving on the ground, I said to him, "Sam, you sit down and rest while I shovel off some of this clay and see what the vein looks like where it is in place."

"All right, I'll take a smoke while you are doing that." I took my pick and began digging. I had been at work only a short time when appearances were so favorable that I concluded to "take a pan." So, taking my crowbar, I began gouging the vein. I had filled the pan about half full when I saw color of gold. "Sam," I called, "I guess we've struck it. There's gold in sight."

"That's bully," said he, and coming over to me, sat down and watched me gouging, the while scratching the clay and quartz in the pan over with a small stick. When I had the pan sufficiently full, I shoved it over to him and said, "Here, Sam, take this over to the pan-hole and wash it, while I take out another."

"Billy," said he, "I wouldn't puddle in that confounded clay for all the gold in Tuolumne County. You pan it; I don't want any of it."

"Very well, Sam, just put it in the pan-hole to soak till I get out this other pan and I'll wash it myself." The result from that first pan was about five dollars in gold, and by quitting time I had panned out about one hundred dollars' worth. So it went for the next ten days, I doing the work and Sam superintending. At the expiration of that time I had extracted all the gold from the pocket, which amounted to about seven hundred dollars. When I received the returns from the mint I proffered Sam one-half of the money as his share as my partner in our mining venture. He refused to take any of it, saying, "The knowledge of mining I acquired while we were taking out that pocket, and the pleasure it gave me, is a better equivalent for my time and labor than that little dab of money."

MARK TWAIN'S BOXING BOUT

Leaving crime and debauchery, gambling and booze fighting behind, I will now go, with my readers, into fairer fields and along pleasanter pathways.

While Mark Twain was reporting on the *Enterprise*, the boys got together and raised enough money to rig up a small gymnasium. Mark, being an expert swordsman, was elected fencing master, and Bruce Garvet, a little Frenchman, teacher of the manly arts of self defense. As Bruce was himself no slouch with the foils, he and Mark gave many exhibitions of their skill with those weapons, all these contests ending with Sam coming out victor.

One evening after Sam had, by a dexterous turn of the wrist, disarmed Bruce, by sending his weapon flying across the room, he stood a few moments gazing in wondering admiration at Sam, then flourishing his hands, made him a bow, saying, "Ah! Meester Clemens, you aire one, grande mastair weeth ze foil. I have nevair weetness zo beautiful work like yours and it gives me great plaisure to have play weeth you, but I theenk if you will with me spar a few rounds, I weel show you that I am your mastair weeth the glove."

Up to this time Sam had always refused to give Bruce satisfaction in a contest with the gloves, saying that it was a brutal sport, and one in which a gentleman should not engage. On this occasion, however, he at last consented to enter the ring for a bout of five rounds. The first two rounds after the men faced each other was occupied in feinting, side stepping and making short jabs to the face and body, neither of them getting in a punch that counted for anything.

In the third round both men began sparring for an opening. Finally Sam, thinking he saw one, rushed and swung for the head, Bruce ducked, stopped the rush, and, with a mighty punch to the nose, lifted Sam from his feet and sent him to the mat, where he lay for a few moments, apparently stunned, with a crimson flood pouring from his nose. Finally raising himself to a sitting posture he gazed, first at one of the boys and then at another, with a surprised, bewildered look, which appeared to ask them what had happened. He at last got to his feet, jerked off the gloves, and throwing them at Bruce, made for the lavatory. After washing the blood from his face and getting into his street clothes, Sam, without turning his head this way or that, stalked out of the gymnasium and crossed the street to Morrill's drug store where Dr. Hammond straightened up his nose. He then went to his room and tumbled into bed.

The next morning his nose was swelled to enormous proportions, and his eyes looked like two slits in a black mask. The first friend he met when he appeared on the street was Paddy Keating, who greeted him with, "Jases! Sam, who the divil throwed the brick?"

"Huh!" grunted Sam, and marched on.

The next man was Charley White, who hailed him with, "Great Scott, Sam, what's that hanging to your face. Come in here and I will unhook it."

"Go to the devil!" snarled Sam, and on he went.

And so it was all along the line. Every friend and acquaintance he met having something to say about his nose.

By the time he reached the *Enterprise* building he was boiling with rage, and forgetting all about breakfast, he went on the jump, up the stairs and into the editorial room and without preface, rasped out. "Joe, I want a month's vacation."

"Oh, you do," said Joe. "Well then, why don't you take it. What have I to say about it? Who are you, anyhow? My friend, I guess you've got into the wrong box."

These words from Joe added fresh fuel to the flame of Sam's wrath and with a mighty blow of his fist upon the table, he almost yelled, "Look here, Joe Goodman, I've had enough of that gaff this morning from the infernal idiots I've met on the way here from my room. You may think it funny, but I don't see it in any such light and I don't want any more of it. And now, I ask you again for a vacation. I won't stay here to have every damn fool in town shoot off his mouth at me, with some kind of rot concerning my nose, and unless you see fit to grant the vacation I ask for, I will leave without it, and if I do, it will be the end of my connection with you and your paper."

When Sam snapped out his ultimatum, Joe began laughing, but when he saw the frown on Sam's face deepening and the angry glint of his eyes, he became serious again and said, "Oh pshaw, Sam, calm yourself and sit down. Of course, you can have a vacation if you want one. Where will you go, and when do you propose to leave?"

"It is a matter of indifference to me as to where I'll go, so that I get away from here. I will leave on the 4 o'clock stage this afternoon."

"Why, Sam, that's the Austin stage. If you are going out that way, it will not interfere with your work on the paper. On the contrary, it will be profitable to both yourself and the *Enterprise*. During your absence from Virginia City you cannot only send a daily letter, but will be able to drum up considerable business for me in the way of ads, bill heads and subscriptions and aside from your regular salary I will pay you a commission on all orders sent in."

Without a goodbye to anyone but Joe and Steve, Sam left that afternoon for Austin.

DAN DEQUILLE FOLLOWS MARK'S NOSE

When the *Enterprise* came out the morning after Mark Twain's departure, an item appeared among the locals, which set the whole town laughing. This was headed—"Who Nose Where It Came From?" and read something like this:

"Just as the stage was about to leave for Austin yesterday, the people who were waiting to see it off were startled out of their equanimity by a strange and most unusual sight. The passengers were in their places and the driver, Billy Watson, had gathered the lines and was just reaching for his whip, when a prodigious, blood red nose was seen to emerge from the office and start for the coach. When it reached the stage and made an attempt to enter the door, two of the lady passengers began screaming with fright at the sight of the dreadful monster, trying to force its way into the coach. The screams of the ladies caused people to come running from all quarters, up and down the street, to learn the cause of the trouble. An excited crowd soon gathered, and it looked for awhile as though a riot would ensue. At this crisis, however, the agent of the company appeared among them and upon his assurance to the passengers that the Nose was perfectly harmless and gentle, their fears were allayed, the Nose was allowed to enter the stage, Billy cracked his whip, and the stage rolled away.—Continued tomorrow."

Every morning for the next two weeks an item something similar to the above appeared in the local columns of the paper. Dan De-Quille trailed Mark's nose along the line of its journey, never mentioning Mark himself—just his nose—giving an account of its enthusiastic reception by the people of all the towns along the way, of the stampeding of bands of cattle and horses, of frightened school children, and its triumphant entrance into Austin, where the Mayor delivered an address of welcome and tendered it the "Freedom of the City."

These articles almost caused the suspension of all business for an hour or two every morning. People meeting on the sidewalks would stop and start talking, laughing and slapping each other on the back in a perfect riot of merriment.

"Old Dan's a corker, ain't he?" would come from one.

"You bet he is," another would answer, "But I'm darned if I'd like to be in his place when Sam gets back. Lord! But wouldn't I like to see Sam now! I'll bet that he's so darned mad that he is dancing a hornpipe all the time. Ha! Ha! Ha!"

Dan's funny writings, causing so much hilarity and mirth to his friends, had a very different effect on Sam. He simply went to pieces with anger, and hurried back to Virginia City with a rush. At about nine o'clock on the night of his return, he entered Goodman's room in a state bordering on insanity and blazed out, "Joe Goodman, whatever in the devil's name possessed you to allow that driveling, half-witted idiot, Dan, to publish his infernal rot about my nose. He has made me the butt of every damn Jack monkey from here to Austin. The confounded ass has got softening of the brain, and I will have no further connection or association with him as a reporter on your paper. If you retain him, I quit, so make your choice."

"Sam," said Joe, "You have worked yourself into a passion which is beyond all reason and common sense. Take a tumble to yourself and think this matter over rationally. Go into the other room and look over the files of the paper for the last six months and you will find that you have made Dan a target for your wit right along. You have stung him pretty hard a good many times, and unmercifully ridiculed him, without a thought regarding his feelings, not caring whether it hurt him or not, just so it put the laugh over on him. Did he ever resent your funny articles at his expense by calling you all the mean things in the dictionary? No, Sir! He never whimpered, but took it all in a spirit of fun, and joined in the laugh at his own expense. And now you are climbing all over yourself because he has come back and put the laugh over on you. Cool down, Sam, and forget it. Forgive old Dan, and don't let this trivial matter cause you to break with him. Let things go on in the same good old way, and we will all be the happier for it."

"You term it a trivial matter, do you? Well, I call it a mean and cowardly attack on me, conceived and written in a spirit of jealousy and spite. I will neither forgive nor forget and I again tell you that I will sever my connection with the paper unless you fire Dan DeQuille."

"This is a tough proposition you are putting up to me, Sam, and I shall have to take time to consider it. I hope that you will also think it over, and after sleeping on it, change your mind."

After his talk with Joe, Sam went into the reporter's room, sat down and filling his pipe, began smoking. Happening to look up at the wall, he spied some copy Dan had left on the hooks. Taking it down, he resumed his seat and began reading the news items in the familiar hand-writing of his old friend, which had been gathered in the earlier part of the evening. He was roused from this occupation by hearing a voice, almost a whisper, saying, "Sam, may I come in?"

Looking up he saw Dan's good old face, with its long goatee and appealing eyes, framed in the partly opened door. The frown upon his face instantly changed to a smile of welcome, and springing to his feet, he shouted, "Open that door Dan, and come in here. You darned old goat, I'm glad to see you."

Then the arms of the two men went around each other, and they began waltzing around the room, knocking over chairs and every other article of furniture that came in their way, bumping against the walls, making such a racket that Steve, fearing that Dan and Sam had gotten into a mixup, hurried to the reporter's room to put a stop to the fracas.

When he opened the door and saw the way Sam and Dan were celebrating their reconciliation, he, too, jumped in and joined in their wild antics. While they were thus whooping things up, Joe came from the other room, and without loss of time, also got into the rumpus. When the jollification ended and quiet was restored, Joe took a check from his pocket and handing it to Sam, said, "Sam, I hate to part with you, but you have left me no alternative. After considering your ultimatum, from every point of view, I find that I cannot possibly comply with your demands. Dan has been with me from the time of the establishment of the *Enterprise* until now. During that time he has filled his position as reporter on the paper so ably and has been such a true and faithful companion and friend that it would be an act of gross injustice, not only to him, but to the whole community as well. Here is a check for your salary, with an additional fifty dollars as a token of my appreciation of your past services."

When Joe presented the check, Sam rasped out, "Don't make a fool of yourself, Joe. Throw that confounded check in the stove, and go back into your room and see if you can, for once in your life, write something with a little common sense in it. Come on, Dan, let's go down town."

And these two funny men walked out, arm in arm.

THE JUMPING FROG STORY

❝ *Well, I don't see no p'ints about that frog that's any better'n any other frog.* **❞**

~ From "The Celebrated Jumping Frog of Calaveras County"

One of the best collections of early Mother Lode stories is *Calaveras County Gold Rush Stories* by Edna Bryan Buckbee. It's filled with remembrances about historic people, places, events, and wonderful descriptions of the Gold Rush days in Calaveras County. The Calaveras Historical Society graciously permitted reproduction of these Buckbee excerpts, along with editor Wallace Motlock's historical commentary.

Of special interest to the history of Sam Clemens is Edna's retelling of the frog jump story and just how Ben Coon told it to Sam in what was then the Lakes Hotel in Angels Camp.

The book is an absolute treasure trove of stories, over 300 entries in the index, each one about those early days in Calaveras County and the people who lived and died there in the pioneer days. And, it's also quite a miracle it was ever published.

Edna died in 1956 and the *Calaveras County Gold Rush Stories* book was first published in 2005, forty-nine years after her passing. Much of the credit for the publication of this book belongs to Mr. Wallace Motlock, a diligent, determined, dedicated historian in these parts, once President of the Calaveras County Historical Society. He describes his "discovery" of her manuscripts in the Introduction to the Calaveras history—Motlock writes:

> While I was hunting for "history nuggets" at the California Historical Society's North Baker Research Library in San Francisco, quite by accident I came

across Mrs. Edna Bryan Buckbee's notes and type-
scripts. I was delighted to find some pertinent information about my own town, Mountain Ranch. Soon
I realized that there, in among the folders and divid-
ers were pieces of a manuscript notes dealing with
"Old Calaveras." It was with a child's excitement that
I searched through files of material that had been donated to the California Historical Society in 1954.
These were not just any stories but local history with
people's names, places and dates, exactly the kind of
Gold Rush narrative I had been hoping to find. This
was a very rich "pay dirt" indeed!

The Tuolumne book was published first but al-
ready in 1932 she had submitted a list of chapters and
an outline to the same publisher for her "Old Calaveras" book. However, in reviewing her letters, there
were problems with the royalty payments from the
publisher for the Tuolumne book. With regards to
the Calaveras book, in a letter to a friend dated October 1935 she writes:

I am heartily sick of Western history, however, I
thank you for your suggestions about "Old Calaveras," but the manuscript, so far as I am concerned,
can furnish paper for lighting this winter's fires.

The publishing company delayed paying her for
three years and in the end they went bankrupt. Financially strapped, Buckbee became bitter and disil-
lusioned.

For various reasons, the "Old Calaveras" manuscript was never turned into a book. Edna died in San

THE JUMPING FROG STORY

Francisco in 1956 and is buried in the Bryan's Plot at People's Cemetery in San Andreas, Calaveras County, the county she loved and knew so well . . . .

Her stories reflect the customs of Gold Rush times. To preserve authenticity, no effort was made to sanitize these or make them more "politically correct." Some of the descriptions of lynchings and murders are gruesome and despicable by today's standards.

Mr. Motlock provides an extensive note of thanks to all of those who helped recover, edit, and fund the publishing of Edna's Calaveras County stories, and we owe an enormous debt of gratitude for their efforts. The following excerpts about the frog jump story are taken from Edna's book, a book whose histories and stories were almost lost forever.

EDNA BUCKBEE AND THE
JUMPING FROG STORY

Included in Edna's remarkable *Calaveras County Gold Rush Stories* is a history of the jumping frog story and Ben Coon's retelling of it to Sam Clemens in Lake's Hotel on that dreary, cold Christmas Eve day. The story is in two parts in the book, and the second part begins after "Knickerbocker Hall." This is probably as close as we will ever get to an accurate narrative of just how the jumping frog story started and Sam Clemens' recording of it.

From Edna's book pages 64-65:

Anyhow, in San Andreas, as early as Don Andreas Pico's time, games of chance seemed naturally a part of the every day existence. Gambling, in all its phases, was indulged in. For instance, wagering their gold on their ability to wing an eagle at long range, "barking" a squirrel, the number of blue-jays shot at the annual jay-hunt, the number of coyote and cougar scalps that would be brought in that season and the number of bears the hunters were likely to trap. Often they gambled for loaves of Mexican bread rather than gold.

Among the sports that resulted in exchanges of gold dust was a frog-jumping contest. It furnished the occasion for the loudest laughter and the greatest amount of fun. Jim Smiley, a Calaveritas gold washer, captured and attempted to train a frog to jump but "Dan'l Webster" failed to win a wager.

This is because Pete Stag, a New York Bowery boy, surreptitiously loaded Smiley's amphibian with buckshot. The loading took place while the unsuspecting gold washer was "up street" at the town pump. Smiley was helping Johnny Ludrun fish out one of the yellow-bellied jumpers that made the pump their headquarters.

Lieutenant Benjamin Ross Coon, of the Home Guards of Angel's (sic) Camp, was a visitor in San Andreas that morning. Later, Ross

Coon, whose flair for a good joke was known all the way from the Cosumnes to the Mariposa rivers, was openly accused with having furnished Pete Stag with both the idea and the buckshot. Smiley's frog, instead of leaping forward, flopped over and died. The scene of Dan'l Webster's or should we say Jim Smiley's humiliation was the middle of Main Street, directly in front of Knickbocker Hall . . . .

From Buckbee's book pages 195-197:

Years later, in his home in San Andreas, Judge Victor Gottschalk told about the defeat of the frog, the "Dan'l Webster" and buckshot that anchored the amphibian to the hard-packed dirt on Main Street. But in spite of its inglorious performance, several years later, the deceased Dan'l's tragedy was capitalized on by Samuel Clemens, whose story, "The Celebrated Jumping Frog of Calaveras County," brought him both fame and riches. Once his book was put into circulation "Sam" Clemens became known to the wide world as the celebrated Mark Twain . . . .

Benjamin Ross Coon, called by his friends "Sly Coon," was as full of pranks as a porcupine's hide is full of spines. He was a dressy young blade, tall, lithe of limb and a living fountain of fun and quick wit. A bartender in C. C. Lake's hotel, he was Angels Camp's champion chess player. Taking Jim Fair's advice, he located a quartz claim near the Crystal claim. Out of the Crystal, recently its owner Jim Fair had scooped in excess of 300 ounces of gold. Ross, besides being a claim owner, was now a lieutenant in the Angels Camp Home Guards, a military organization of which Philip Scribner was the Captain.

Ross Coon of Angels Camp had the "two bit" habit, which is to say, that to him a nickel was worthless, not even a "chicken feed." He carried this off on the grounds that it would be destructive to his high standard of living to be otherwise. Ross Coon was called "High Old Coon" because he refused to recognize the lowly nickel as legal tender. Be this as it may, he was a raconteur of the first order, a sort of bugle-horn for Angels Hotel.

The Bear Mountain Range was wearing a mantle of snow on the 24th day of December, 1863, [other sources list this at 1864]when a buckboard drawn by a span of blood bays rumbled down Hanselman's Hill to Campo de los Muertos and onward to Angels Camp. The occupants, Jim Gills, Dick Stoker, and their guest, Sam Clemens, they had a long and cold ride that day. The tramp from Jackass Hill to Tuttletown hadn't been any too easy either. The buckboard ride from Tuttletown, Tuolumne County, down the steep, crooked slumgullion road to Robinson's Ferry, thence up the rocky, rutted hill to Carson Creek and onward to Lake's Hotel in Angels Camp was anything but soothing. Small wonder that these friends, out to spend a pleasant holiday, were alighted stiff of knee and chilled to the bone.

Upon entering Lake's Barroom they saw hanging near the large iron stove, water-soaked woolen caps and felt hats. In the room the odor of rubber and elk skin mingled freely with that of tobacco, Old Bourbon and other equally well-known brands. At the card tables, in friendly games sat William Coddington, George Tryon, Jacob Caster, Ben Strauss, Jim Anderson, Bob Patterson, Phil Scribner, Jim Fair, Jack Crooks, John Gardner, and Doctor Kelly. Evergreen wreaths hung from the inside of windows, Tom and Jerry flowed freely and in fact the barroom was filled with Christmas cheer.

After the storm-coated trio had refreshed themselves at the bar, Ross Coon, who was off duty that afternoon, stopped in the middle of a chess game with Bill Finnegan, got up, straightened his velvet vest and gave the guests from the south side of the Stanislaus River, a right royal greeting.

Old Alex, the town-crier, dozing near the stove awakened and blinked red-rimmed eyes when Sam Clemens and his companions seated themselves in hickory chairs, lighted their pipes and prepared to enjoy a peaceful smoke. Old Alex, perceiving their desire for quiet, left the scene for the street. No sooner had his back been turned, than Ross Coon drew a chair close to the visitors and by way of entertainment related the story of a frog, named Dan'l Webster. This frog had failed to win a wager for its trainer, Jim Smiley of Calaveritas because while its owner was at the town pump, a couple of smart alecks loaded the yellow-bellied jumper with buckshot.

The droll, inimitable way that Ross' voice drifted through the yarn and his apparent complete approval of the way in which Sam Seabough had written it, was of interest to Sam Clemens, who thought the story of a jumping frog, however well related was absurd. A moment later, Old Alex returned to the barroom with news of a lunar rainbow, a rare sight in Angels Camp. His curiosity whetted, Sam Clemens went outdoors and looked skyward at the Gossamer band of light, a sort of promise of good fortune.

A short time later, when Sam Clemens picked up a billiard cue to send ivory balls over green felt in a game of pool with Jim Gillis, he kept hearing in his imagination, Ross Coon mimic Pete Stagg, of the buckshot artists:

"I ain't got no frog, but if I had a frog I'd bet you."

Ross Coon's narration of a newspaper story, at the time seemed unimportant, but later it proved to be the nucleus around which an unsurpassed fame was built. Other treasure piles in Calaveras County have yielded golden nuggets, but none so sparkling as the one creviced out of a news sheet in the barroom of Lake's Hotel on Christmas Eve in 1863. The great literary nugget was published under the title "The Celebrated Jumping Frog of Calaveras County," and Sam Clemens became, to the wide world, the celebrated Mark Twain.

$\mathcal{T}he$

BOOMERANG ARTICLE

$\mathcal{E}$

The Celebrated Jumping Frog of Calaveras County

The "*Boomerang*" article and "The Celebrated Jumping
Frog of Calaveras County" are reprinted here with the permission
of the Mark Twain Papers and Project of the Bancroft Library,
University of California, Berkeley

In 2010, the Angels Camp Museum, with the guidance of then
Director Bob Rogers, created and dedicated a new exhibit, "Mark
Twain Explores the American Dream," which tells the story of
Twain's journey to Angels Camp and his becoming the famous
writer we all admire.

The exhibit was created with the assistance of Dr. Gregg Camfield,
author of *The Oxford Companion to Mark Twain*, (2003) and his
students from U. C. Merced. He and his students spent months
conducting research and provided the museum with all the neces-
sary documentation for the world-class exhibit.

THE BOOMERANG ARTICLE

The Mark Twain Papers and Projects at the Bancroft Library, University of California, Berkeley, Mr. Robert Hirst, General Editor, and Mr. Victor Fisher, Associate Editor, were very helpful in providing photos and other Mark Twain resources to the museum project. Over 20 original photos, including the very first daguerreotype ever taken of San Clemens at the age of 15, were donated, and all manner of original letters, documents, and writings were made available to be placed on display.

Along with the exhibit, a book, *The Five Jumps of the Calaveras Frog*, was produced as well. It is the only book that includes all five stories that Mark Twain wrote about the jumping frog and Angels Camp. The museum obtained permission from the Mark Twain Papers and Project and the Bancroft Library to publish these stories as a collection for the very first time.

Two stories, "Boomerang" and "The Celebrated Jumping Frog of Calaveras County," in the *Five Jumps* book are reprinted here with the permission of the Mark Twain Papers and Project of the Bancroft Library.

Mark Twain wrote the following account of Boomerang. There was no such town, but, since he was in Angels Camp, it is believed to be representative of Tuttletown and Angels Camp, which he first saw in the winter of 1864 and wrote about in his *Autobiography* and *Roughing It*. By that time, the golden days of the Gold Rush were over, but Billy Gillis described Tuttletown in its heyday, not unlike the picture Mark Twain paints here about Boomerang's past: "Their streets were crowded with stores and shops, and the stores and shops were thronged with hurrying, excited customers."

What follows is the story written by Mark Twain describing the town of Boomerang.

THE ONLY RELIABLE ACCOUNT OF
THE CELEBRATED JUMPING FROG OF CALAVERAS COUNTY
Article by Mark Twain

TOGETHER WITH SOME REFERENCE TO THE DECAYING CITY
OF BOOMERANG, AND A FEW GENERAL REMARKS
CONCERNING MR. SIMON WHEELER, A RESIDENT OF THE SAID
CITY IN THE DAY OF ITS GRANDEUR.

In accordance with your request I herewith furnish you with a report of the present condition and appearance of the once flourishing mining town of Boomerang, to supply a vacancy which must necessarily occur in the history of your travels in consequence of your having neglected to travel in that direction.

Also, in accordance with your instructions, I made the acquaintance of Simon Wheeler, the venerable rural historian, who resided at Boomerang in early times, (though for years past he has lived in unostentatious privacy on the picturesque borders of Lake Tulare) and obtained from him a just and true account of the celebrated Jumping Frog of Calaveras County for your pages.

EN ROUTE FOR BOOMERANG

I traveled from here toward Boomerang by steamboat a part of the way, and took the stage early the next morning. All day long we slopped through the mud, over a monotonous plain, with eyes fixed on the gleaming snows of the distant Sierras, and dreary enough the journey was. About every five miles we encountered a rickety weather-beaten farm-house, and then sketched and re-sketched its dismal outlines in imagination until we came to the next one—which was always a more dilapidated one the further we proceeded inland—and finally when the tedious sun went down, my mind's eye presented no panorama of the day's travel but two long lines of staggering fences, interrupted at stated intervals by desolate cabins, with here and there a melancholy dog or a broken-hearted cow. I was glad to see the day close in. I was glad there was no Joshua there to command the sun to stand still.

BOOMERANG - PAST

I staid (sic) in Boomerang five or six days. In it there are probably twenty crazy houses occupied and thirty still crazier ones tenantless. The stream that flows through the middle of the town winds its tortuous course through symmetrical piles of pebbles and boulders that had passed through the gold miner's sluice boxes years ago and were dumped into the positions they now occupy. In those days this stream swarmed with men of every nationality under the sun, and some took out a thousand dollars a day and none less than thirty or forty. At night they collected in splendid saloons, in their savage-looking costumes, and gambled away moderate fortunes, and got drunk on costly foreign liquors, and dissected each other with eighteen-inch bowie-knives in their frank, off-hand way, and all were gay and happy.

They rolled ten-pins; they played billiards; they indulged in expensive balls; they ordered elegant suppers, and ate them and paid for them; they turned out on great occasions in grand dress parade—firemen, soldiers, benevolent societies and had silken banners, and walked under gorgeous triumphal arches and fulminated their sentiments from thundering cannon. They had a newspaper and a telegraph, and talked of a railroad. They never quite reached to the dignity of supporting a Board of Aldermen, but they had a sort of semi-responsible body of Trustees and a Mayor. And also an entirely responsible but inefficient police force consisting of a constable. Their streets were crowded with stores and shops, and the stores and shops were thronged with hurrying, excited customers.

BOOMERANG - PRESENT

Behold the Boomerang of to-day! Where the stream formerly swarmed with bearded miners, five skinny, long-tailed Chinamen shovel and sluice starvation wages out of the poverty-stricken banks of pebbles. Where splendid saloons once collected the cheerful multitudes to gamble and drink and carve each other, a solitary, dilapidated gin-mill gapes hungrily for customers and finds them not. There are no banquets, no ten-pins, no bails, in Boomerang to-day. Dejected stragglers mope where grand processions marched before; and they invoke the ghost of their departed splendor in inexpensive gin, and pop their patriotism from an anvil on the Fourth of July. They have no newspaper and no telegraph, and the railroad is a forgotten dream. The Board of Trustees have wandered to distant lands, and the inefficient constable is dead. The streets that were crowded with stores and shops are desolate, and the throngs that bought and sold in them have gone away toward the rising sun. Lo! thy pride is humbled, thy hopes are blighted, the day of thy glory hath departed, and thy history is even as the history of a human life, O Boomerang!

Well, you can hardly realize such extraordinary changes. Yonder is a dwelling house that was new and rather handsome ten years ago, and cost five thousand dollars unfurnished. The owner would take two hundred and fifty for it to-day. Here is a house that once had a piano in it, and also a young lady. A piano and a young lady where now is nought but a wide-spread epidemic of unpainted old tenements, surrounded by discouraged gardens reveling in weeds!

Town-lots in Boomerang were once sold by the front foot and at extravagant prices, but now they are offered by the acre and not sold at all.

At the very same restaurant in Boomerang where men once feasted on costly imported delicacies and stimulated their appetites with rich foreign wines, you must put up with beans and bacon, now, and wash them down with muddy coffee.

The sole remaining saloon is kept by a man who tries honestly to make a living out of his own custom, because he has no other to speak of. True, Calvin Smith used to come down from Horsefly once a month and get drunk, but here lately he has grown so irregular that there is no dependence to be placed in him. The saloon-keeper awoke to this fact too late and couldn't sell out, because Smith's custom constituted the "good-will" of the concern, and who would buy a gin-mill whose good-will was so manifestly irregular as this?

The single billiard table in that saloon is a relic of former times. The "counters" are so fly-blown that you cannot tell the white string from the black one; the table-cover is faded, and threadbare, and is patched in a dozen places; one of the pockets is bottomless; the cues arc warped like willow fishing-rods and the leathers on them are worn as hard and smooth as trunk-nails; if you get the "warp" of your cue right, you stand some chance of getting your "English" on the side you want it on—but if you don't you can depend on accomplishing the reverse; none but old citizens who have stuck to the town and "kept the hang" of those cues from the first can hit the balls with them at all, I think or at any rate do it every time without fail. Concerning the balls I may say that to an outsider there is no perceptible difference between them as to color; true, there is a bare suspicion of red on two of them, but if you look fixedly at the other two you will infallibly imagine there is a suspicion of red on them also, and so when strangers play the ruined and melancholy bar-keeper will come forward from time to time, as necessity requires, and decide with unspeakable solemnity which is the "dark red," and which the "pale," and which is the "spot" ball and which isn't, and then retire slowly behind his bar with the air of a man who considers human knowledge as vain and little worth when the proud soul is borne down by a royal despair. And if you recklessly hint that the "dark red" of his decision is really the "pale," how his watery eye withers you with its lofty compassion! —as who should say, "I have handled them for fifteen years, poor ignorant worm!" These remarkable balls are chipped and scarred and cracked and blistered beyond all power of conception, and when they are under way they bounce and scamper and clatter as if they had cogs on them. I never saw a man make a "shot" on that table that he tried to make, but I did see shots made which Phelan and Kavanaugh would unhesitatingly pronounce impossible. You might drive one of those balls against another, for instance; your ball bounds to the left we will say; it glances from a rough seam in the cloth and flies back to the right; it staggers against a patch and goes off to the left again; it gets into a rut in the table and rolls ten inches in a straight line in defiance of all rules of philosophy to the contrary; it strikes the angle of a patch and returns to the right once more, and closes its extraordinary career within half an inch of the "dark red;" very well, you think you haven't "counted"—but just as the thought crosses your mind, your ball, which has only balanced for an instant on one of the warts on its surface, "keels over" in consequence of a gouged place on its under side, and touches the "dark red!" There are no miracles like that laid down in Mr. Phelan's hand-book of billiards.

I seem to have wandered from my subject somewhat. However, no matter—if your readers can't tell by intuition what a town looks like which not only tolerates but is perfectly satisfied with a billiard table like that, it would be a waste of labor on my part to try to describe it to them intelligibly; and if they can't form a correct estimate of the enterprise of a community where only liquor enough is drank to support one barkeeper and that barkeeper has to drink that liquor himself, it would be presumption in mine to try to furnish an estimate they could hope to understand. I am not inspired—let me pass on to [...]

BOOMERANG - FUTURE

The real wealth of Boomerang is still in the bowels of the earth. The town is surrounded by a network of the richest gold-bearing lodes in California—lodes which, when thoroughly opened, will produce more bullion in six months than the Boomerangers washed from the gulches in fifteen years. The ancient magnificence of Boomerang will yet return to her with a doubled and redoubled lustre she dreams not of to-day. But will the disconsolate barkeeper profit by these things? Will the 5 skinny Chinamen become Mandarins of two tails and inexhaustible cash? Will the seedy stragglers—the gin-soaking, anvil-bursting dreamers—be exalted and arrayed in the purple and fine linen of the new empire? No—they have sold their birthright for a mess of pottage and a New York company has bought it. Alas! poor Boomerangers! in the fulness of time you will wake up some day and be astonished!

A miner's shack, with Peter Meyers and his wife, Mary, in North Branch, circa 1907. Photo courtesy of Calaveras County Historical Society

Illustration by Frederick Waddy, first appeared in Harper's Weekly
Courtesy of the Mark Twain Project—The Bancroft Library,
University of California, Berkeley

The following version of the jumping frog story is in its slightly revised form published in Mark Twain's first book in 1867.

THE CELEBRATED JUMPING FROG OF CALAVERAS COUNTY

By Mark Twain

In compliance with the request of a friend of mine, who wrote me from the East, I called on good-natured, garrulous old Simon Wheeler, and inquired after my friend's friend, Leonidas W. Smiley, as requested to do, and I here unto append the result. I have a lurking suspicion that Leonidas W. Smiley is a myth; that my friend never knew such a personage; and that he only conjectured that, if I asked old Wheeler about him, it would remind him of his infamous Jim Smiley, and he would go to work and bore me nearly to death with some infernal reminiscence of him as long and tedious as it should be useless to me. If that was the design, it certainly succeeded.

I found Simon Wheeler dozing comfortably by the bar-room stove of the old, dilapidated tavern in the ancient mining camp of Angel's, and I noticed that he was fat and bald-headed, and had an expression of winning gentleness and simplicity upon his tranquil countenance. He roused up and gave me good-day. I told him a friend of mine had commissioned me to make some inquiries about a cherished companion of his boyhood named Leonidas W. Smiley—Rev. Leonidas W. Smiley—a young minister of the Gospel, who he had heard was at one time a resident of Angel's Camp. I added that, if Mr. Wheeler could tell me any thing about this Rev. Leonidas W. Smiley, I would feel under many obligations to him.

Simon Wheeler backed me into a corner and blockaded me there with his chair, and then sat me down and reeled off the monotonous narrative which follows this paragraph. He never smiled, he never frowned, he never changed his voice from the gentle-flowing key to which he tuned the initial sentence, he never betrayed the slightest suspicion of enthusiasm; but all through the interminable narrative there ran a vein of impressive earnestness and sincerity, which showed me plainly that, so far from his imagining that there was any thing ridiculous or funny about his story, he regarded it as a really important matter, and admired its two heroes as men of transcendent genius in finesse. To me, the spectacle of a man drifting serenely along through such a queer yarn without ever smiling, was exquisitely absurd. As I said before, I asked him to tell me what he knew of Rev. Leonidas W. Smiley, and he replied as follows. I let him go on in his own way, and never interrupted him once:

There was a feller here once by the name of Jim Smiley, in the winter of '49 or may be it was the spring of '50 I don't recollect exactly, somehow, though what makes me think it was one or the other is because I remember the big flume wasn't finished when he first came to the camp; but any way, he was the curiosest man about always betting on any thing that turned up you ever see, if he could get any body to bet on the other side; and if he couldn't, he'd change sides. Any way that suited the other man would suit him any way just so's he got a bet, he was satisfied. But still he was lucky, uncommon lucky; he most always come out winner. He was always ready and laying for a chance; there couldn't be no solittry thing mentioned but that feller'd offer to bet on it, and take any side you please, as I was just telling you. If there was a horse-race, you'd find him flush, or you'd find him busted at the end of it; if there was a dog-fight, he'd bet on it; if there was a cat-fight, he'd bet on it; if there was a chicken-fight, he'd bet on it; why, if there was two birds setting on a fence, he would bet you which one would fly first; or if there was a camp-meeting, he would be there reg'lar, to bet on Parson Walker, which he judged to be the best exhorter about here, and so he was, too, and a good man. If he even seen a straddle-bug start to go anywheres, he would bet you how long it would take him to get wherever he was going to, and if you took him up, he would foller that straddle-bug to Mexico but what he would find out where he was bound for and how long he was on the road. Lots of the boys here has seen that Smiley, and can tell you about him. Why, it never made no difference to him he would bet on any thing the dangdest feller. Parson Walker's wife laid very sick once, for a good while, and it seemed as if they warn's going to save her; but one morning he come in, and Smiley asked how she was, and he said she was considerable better thank the Lord for his inftnit mercy and coming on so smart that, with the blessing of Providence, she'd get well yet; and Smiley, before he thought, says, "Well, I'll risk two-and-a-half that she don't, any way."

Thish-yer Smiley had a mare the boys called her the fifteen-minute nag, but that was only in fun, you know, because, of course, she was faster than that and he used to win money on that horse, for all she was so slow and always had the asthma, or the distemper, or the consumption, or something of that kind. They used to give her two or three hundred yards start, and then pass her under way; but always at the fag-end of the race she'd get excited and desperate-like, and come cavorting and straddling up, and scattering her legs around limber, sometimes in the air, and sometimes out to one side amongst the fences, and kicking up m-o-r-e dust, and raising m-o-r-e racket with her coughing and sneezing and blowing her nose and always fetch up at the stand just about a neck ahead, as near as you could cipher it down.

And he had a little small bull pup, that to look at him you'd think he wan's worth a cent, but to set around and look ornery, and lay for a chance to steal something. But as soon as money was up on him, he was a different dog; his underjaw'd begin to stick out like the fo'castle of a steamboat, and his teeth would uncover, and shine savage like the furnaces. And a dog might tackle him, and bully-rag him, and bite him, and throw him over his shoulder two or three times, and

Andrew Jackson which was the name of the pup Andrew Jackson would never let on but what he was satisfied, and hadn't expected nothing else and the bets being doubled and doubled on the other side all the time, till the money was all up; and then all of a sudden he would grab that other dog jest by the j'int of his hind leg and freeze on it not chew, you understand, but only jest grip and hang on till they thronged up the sponge, if it was a year. Smiley always come out winner on that pup, till he harnessed a dog once that didn't have no hind legs, because they'd been sawed off by a circular saw, and when the thing had gone along far enough, and the money was all up, and he come to make a snatch for his pet bolt, he saw in a minute how he'd been imposed on, and how the other dog had him in the door, so to speak, and he 'peered surprised, and then he looked sorter discouraged-like, and didn't try no more to win the fight, and so he got shucked out bad. He give Smiley a look, as much as to say his heart was broke, and it was his fault, for putting up a dog that hadn't no hind legs for him to take bolt of, which was his main dependence in a fight, and then he limped off a piece and laid down and died. It was a good pup, was that Andrew Jackson, and would have made a name for hisself if he'd lived, for the stuff was in him, and he had genius I know it, because he hadn't had no opportunities to speak of, and it don't stand to reason that a dog could make such a fight as he could under them circumstances, if he hadn't no talent. It always makes me feel sorry when I think of that last fight of his'n, and the way it turned out.

Well, thish-yer Smiley had rat-tarriers, and chicken cocks, and tomcats, and all of them kind of things, till you couldn't rest, and you couldn't fetch nothing for him to bet on but he'd match you. He ketched a frog one day, and took him home, and said he cal'klated to edercate him; and so he never done nothing for three months but set in his back yard and learn that frog to jump. And you bet you he did learn him, too. He'd give him a little punch behind, and the next minute you'd see that frog whirling in the air like a doughnut see him turn one summerset, or may be a couple, if he got a good start, and come down flat-footed and all right, like a cat. He got him up so in the matter of catching flies, and kept him in practice so constant, that he'd nail a fly every time as far as he could see him. Smiley said all a frog wanted was education, and he could do most any thing and I believe him. Why, I've seen him set Dan'l Webster down here on this floor Dan'l Webster was the name of the frog and sing out, "Flies, Dan'l, flies!" and quicker'n you could wink, he'd spring straight up, and snake a fly off'n the counter there, and flop down on the floor again as solid as a gob of mud, and fall to scratching the side of his head with his hind foot as indifferent as if he hadn't no idea he'd been doin' any more'n any frog might do. You never see a frog so modest and straightforward as he was, for all he was so gifted. And when it come to fair and square jumping on a dead level, he could get over more ground at one straddle than any animal of his breed you ever see. Jumping on a dead level was his strong suit, you understand; and when it come to that, Smiley would ante up money on him as long as he had a red. Smiley was monstrous proud of his frog, and well he might be, for fellers that had traveled and been everywheres, all said he laid over any frog that ever they see.

Well, Smiley kept the beast in a little lattice box, and he used to fetch him down town sometimes and lay for a bet. One day a feller a stranger in the camp, he was come across him with his box, and says:

"What might it be that you've got in the box?"

And Smiley says, sorter indifferent like, "It might be a parrot, or it might be a canary, may be, but it an't it's only just a frog."

And the feller took it, and looked at it careful, and turned it round this way and that, and says, "H'm so 'tis. Well, what's he good for?"

"Well," Smiley says, easy and careless, "He's good enough for one thing, I should judge he can outjump any frog in Calaveras county."

The feller took the box again, and took another long, particular look, and give it back to Smiley, and says, very deliberate, "Well, I don't see no p'ints about that frog that's any better'n any other frog."

"May be you don't," Smiley says. "May be you understand frogs, and may be you don't understand 'em; may be you've had experience, and may be you an't only a amature, as it were. Anyways, I've got my opinion, and I'll risk forty dollars that he can outjump any frog in Calaveras county."

And the feller studied a minute, and then says, kinder sad like, "Well, I'm only a stranger here, and I an't got no frog; but if I had a frog, I'd bet you."

And then Smiley says, "That's all right that's all right if you'll hold my box a minute, I'll go and get you a frog." And so the feller took the box, and put up his forty dollars along with Smiley's, and set down to wait.

So he set there a good while thinking and thinking to hisself, and then he got the frog out and prized his mouth open and took a tea-spoon and filled him full of quail shot filled him pretty near up to his chin and set him on the floor. Smiley he went to the swamp and slopped around in the mud for a long time, and finally he ketched a frog, and fetched him in, and give him to this feller, and says: "Now, if you're ready, set him alongside of Dan'l, with his fore-paws just even with Dan'l, and I'll give the word." Then he says, "One two three jump!" and him and the feller touched up the frogs from behind, and the new frog hopped off, but Dan'l give a heave, and hysted up his shoulders so like a Frenchman, but it wan's no use he couldn't budge; he was planted as solid as an anvil, and he couldn't no more stir than if he was anchored out. Smiley was a good deal surprised, and he was disgusted too, but he didn't have no idea what the matter was, of course.

142

The feller took the money and started away; and when he was going out at the door, he sorter jerked his thumb over his shoulders this way at Dan'l, and says again, very deliberate, "Well, I don't see no p'ints about that frog that's any better'n any other frog."

Smiley he stood scratching his head and looking down at Dan'l a long time, and at last he says, "I do wonder what in the nation that frog throw'd off for I wonder if there an't something the matter with him he 'pears to look mighty baggy, somehow." And he ketched Dan'l by the nap of the neck, and lifted him up and says, "Why, blame my cats, if he don't weigh five pound!" and turned him upside down, and he belched out a double handful of shot. And then he see how it was, and he was the maddest man he set the frog down and took out after that feller, but he never ketchd him. And—

[Here Simon Wheeler heard his name called from the front yard, and got up to see what was wanted.] And turning to me as he moved away, he said: "Just set where you are, stranger, and rest easy I an't going to be gone a second."

But, by your leave, I did not think that a continuation of the history of the enterprising vagabond Jim Smiley would be likely to afford me much information concerning the Rev. Leonidas W. Smiley, and so I started away.

At the door I met the sociable Wheeler returning, and he buttonholed me and recommenced:

"Well, thish-yer Smiley had a yeller one-eyed cow that didn't have no tail, only jest a short stump like a bannanner, and[—]"

"Oh! hang Smiley and his afflicted cow!" I muttered, good-naturedly, and bidding the old gentleman good-day, I departed.

THE LEGACY OF THE
JUMPING FROG STORY

*"On Your Mark" photo by Susie Hoffman, Copperopolis, CA
From the 2014 Calaveras County Fair and Frog Jumping Jubilee*

Each year, thousands head for Angels Camp to attend the four-day Calaveras County Fair & Jumping Frog Jubilee, held in mid-May, which averages an annual attendance of 37,000 people. Along with over 7,000 exhibits, rodeos, horse events, and all manner of entertainments, the greatest attraction continues to be the annual frog jump contest, a four-day event concluding in the awarding of a grand champion after Sunday afternoon's closing competition. A handsome brass plaque commemorating the winner is annually embedded in the sidewalk of downtown Angels Camp. This "Frog Hop of Fame" is engraved with the name of the winning jockey, frog and leaping distance for three jumps.

Downtown Angels Camp clothesline display indicating the coming of the Calaveras County Fair Jumping Frog Jubilee. Photo by Connie Strawbridge

A replica of Mark Twain's Cabin rolls down Main Street in an early Jumping Frog Jubilee Parade. Photos courtesy of Angels Camp Museum.

The Jumping Frog Jubilee is the largest, most impressive attribution the region has which honors the legacy of Mark Twain and the time he spent in the Mother Lode. The Angels Camp Hotel is where Ben Coon told Twain the story about Jim Smiley and his frog, Dan'l Webster. Twain would take that short entry in his new notebook, "Number 4", and turn it into "Jim Smiley and His Jumping Frog," published in 1865 with the pen name Mark Twain. That story made Twain famous on a national level and future works like *Innocents Abroad, Roughing It, Adventures of Tom Sawyer*, and *Adventures of Huckleberry Finn* would make him one of the world's most celebrated writers.

There has been, and always will be, a connection between the memory of Twain's fame and Dan'l Webster, the frog that Jim Smiley thought could never be beaten. But, as Twain writes, "The feller took the money and started away; and when he was going out at the door, he sorter jerked his thumb over his shoulders this way at Dan'l, and says again, very deliberate, "Well, I don't see no p'ints about that frog that's any better'n any other frog."

BOOMERANG, PAST AND PRESENT

In writing "Boomerang," Mark Twain suggests that the real wealth of the town was down in the ground:

> The real wealth of Boomerang is still in the bowels of the earth. The town is surrounded by a network of the richest gold-bearing lodes in California—lodes which, when thoroughly opened, will produce more bullion in six months than the Boomerangers washed from the gulches in fifteen years. The ancient magnificence of Boomerang will yet return to her with a doubled and redoubled lustre she dreams not of today.

And, for over 20 to 30 years, that's what happened. Hard rock mines like Angels, Lightner, Gold Cliff and Utica drilled down over 3,000 feet and carved at least 200 miles of tunnels beneath Angels Camp. But, just as in the old Gold Rush days of Billy Gillis, the gold would run out, and no hard rock mines would reopen in Angels Camp after WWII. Once again, miners and fortune seekers would have to find other ways to make a living.

Lightner Mine: Closed 1915. Photo Courtesy of Calaveras County Historical Society

Utica Mine: Closed 1916. Photo Courtesy of Calaveras County Historical Society

Angels Mine: Closed 1918. Photo Courtesy of Calaveras County Historical Society

Gold Cliff: Closed 1920. Photo Courtesy of Calaveras County Historical Society

A NEW GOLD RUSH IN THE MOTHER LODE

Beginning in the 1960s and 1970s, new major subdivisions along Highways 4 and 49, like La Contenta, Saddle Creek, Greenhorn Creek, Forest Meadows, Blue Lake Springs, and Big Trees Village, attracted many new people fleeing the stress of city living. Recreational areas such as Bear Valley Ski Resort, Calaveras Big Trees State Park, caverns, rafting, camping, and all manner of outdoor activities above the fog have attracted many new residents and visitors to the Mother Lode. Throughout the 1990s, Calaveras County's population more than doubled as people migrated from cities to the quiet countryside offering a rural way of life.

Along with residents and recreation came a new industry, winemaking. Stevenot Winery was the first to be developed in the region, and in the early 1970s, Cabernet Sauvignon, Chardonnay, and Zinfandel vines were planted. An old hay barn was converted into a winery, and the first 2,200 cases were released in 1979. What followed was another rush to the Gold Country as vintners migrated to the Mother Lode to mine a different kind of gold—one that grew right out of the ground. Milliaire, Black Sheep, Indian Rock, Kautz Ironstone, and Chatom were all in operation by 1996 when 260 acres were planted in grapes. Currently, there are more than 20 members of the Calaveras Winegrape Alliance with over 1,000 acres in production.

The region is rich in recreation, charming shops, museums of Gold Rush history, and is home to the famous Frog Jump. There is much to explore in this historic, majestic, bountiful region. The real value of the Mother Lode lies in its natural beauty and the inspiration it provides.

Having been Twain's retreat from the trials and troubles of the day, the Mother Lode became a treasure trove he would mine for the rest of his literary career. Mark Twain's journey to Jackass Hill and Angels Camp had escape at its core, but after spending 88 days, he used a colorful local story about a frog to launch his fame, fortune, and legacy as one of America's greatest writers.

As Mark Twain advises ~

" *Eat a live frog first thing in the morning and nothing worse will happen to you the rest of the day.* **"**

MEET STORYTELLER &
AUTHOR, JAMES FLETCHER
aka "MINER JIM"

*Mark Twain in bronze at the entrance to Camps Restaurant, Greenhorn Creek
Resort, Angels Camp. Photo by Connie Strawbridge*

Jim Fletcher was born in the logging community of Vernonia,
Oregon, in the heart of cool and rainy Douglas fir country. He grad-
uated from Vernonia High School and attended what is now Western Oregon University, receiving his education degree in 1966.

He came south in search of sunshine to teach at Turlock High
School where he met and married his wife of 35 years, Sandra Neu-
bauer Fletcher. In 1972 he took a position as Vice Principal at Roo-
sevelt Junior High School in Modesto, California. He moved to La
Loma Junior High in 1988, and returned to the classroom as an in-
structor of 7th grade social studies and language arts where he remained until his retirement in 2005.

151

Jim has two sons—Eric who lives in Modesto—and Robert, living in Oakland. His first wife Sandra passed away in 2004. The family loved the mountains and spent many winters at Bear Valley skiing, hiking, and enjoying snowy or sunny days. Every summer they spent a week at the Ridge Tahoe, a place he still loves to visit today. For him, like Mark Twain, there is something energizing about mountain country and lake vistas.

Jim married Kristin Cromwell in 2006 and they reside in Angels Camp, California. He was a docent at the Angels Camp Museum for many years and helped put the pole barn and hard rock mining exhibits together. Jim loved to talk to groups of kids and adults about geology, gold panning, and hard rock mining. Now, he loves spending wonderful days leading tours of the North Grove of Calaveras Big Trees State Park, just up the road on Highway 4. As "Miner Jim" he continues his weekly programs at Camps Restaurant, sharing the life of Mark Twain and those very special 88 days he spent on Jackass Hill.

Sam Clemens/Mark Twain
Calendar of Western Adventures

John C. Brown and Bert Simonis, owners, directors, and producers for This 'n That Films, created a documentary film, *88 Days in the Mother Lode, Mark Twain Finds His Voice,* a wonderful recreation of Sam's coming to the West and the significance of his 88-day stay on Jackass Hill. Included in the materials on their website is a calendar of his time in the West, and a slightly edited version is presented here.

THE 88-DAY STORY TIMELINE

14 August 1861 – Arrives in Carson City with his brother Orion Clemens who is Secretary to the Territory of Nevada

September 1862 – Arrives in Virginia City and goes to work for the *Territorial Enterprise.* "He reached Virginia City in September 1862, in his own estimation a 'rusty looking specimen,' coatless, slouch hat, blue woolen shirt, pantaloons stuffed into boot-tops, whiskered half down to the waist, and the universal navy revolver slung to my belt."

3 February 1863 – Signs a newspaper article for the first time as Mark Twain at the *Territorial Enterprise*

22 December 1863 – Artemus Ward comes to Virginia City to lecture; stays for 11 days

June 1864 – Arrives in San Francisco

30 November 1864 – Samuel L. Clemens quietly celebrates his 29th birthday

1 December 1864 – Lives in San Francisco at 44 Minna Street in a boarding house run by Martha Gillis—leaves for Sonora/Jackass Hill by steamer/stagecoach through Stockton

4 December 1864 – Arrives in Jackass Hill

31 December 1864 – Spends New Year's Eve in Vallecito with Jim Gillis

22 January 1865 – Travels from Jackass Hill to Angels Camp

Late January 1865 – Hears the story of the Jumping Frog of Calaveras County as told by Ben Coon, bartender and former river boat pilot, while hiding out from the rain in Angels Hotel.

8 February 1865 – Attends Masonic meeting in Angels Camp

20 February 1865 – Returns to Jackass Hill

23 February 1865 – Leaves for San Francisco via Copperopolis and Stockton

26 February 1865 – Arrives at Occidental Hotel in San Francisco—finds a letter from Artemus Ward asking for a story for his book about tales in the West

September 1865 – Dreams about the Jumping Frog story and writes first draft

8 October 1865 – Writes about a 6.5 earthquake in San Francisco

18 October 1865 – Sends "Jim Smiley and his Jumping Frog of Calaveras County" story to Artemus Ward

19 October 1865 – Sends a letter to Orion and Mollie, in pencil on the back: You are in trouble, & in debt—so am I. I am utterly miserable—so are you. Perhaps your religion will sustain you, will feed you—I place no dependence in mine. Our religions are alike, though, in one respect—neither can make a man happy when he is out of luck. If I do not get out of debt in 3 months,—pistols or poison for one—exit me.

18 November 1865 – "The Jumping Frog of Calaveras County" is published by the *New York Saturday Press* and is copied by newspaper editors throughout the East Coast.

30 November, 1865 – Samuel L. Clemens turns thirty

Early 1866 – Starts working for the *Sacramento Daily Union*

March 1866 – Takes steamship Ajax to Sandwich Islands He's a correspondent for the *Sacramento Daily Union*, the largest newspaper on the West Coast.

13 August 1866 – Returns by sailing ship to San Francisco

2 October 1866 – First lecture - Maguire's Academy of Music in San Francisco - Sacramento (11 October), Marysville (15 October), Grass Valley (20 October), Nevada City (23 October), Red Dog (24 October), and You Bet (25 October).

30 October 1866 – Gives a lecture in Virginia City

30 November 1866 – Samuel Clemens turns thirty-one

15 December 1866 – Sails for New York

Calendar Copyright @ 2015 This 'n That Films

Works Cited

Branch, Edgar Marquess, Robert H. Hirst, Harriet Elinor Smith, eds.
Early Tales and Sketches, Volume 2, 1864-1865. Berkeley, CA: University of
California Press, 1981. Print.

Brown, John C. and Bert Simonis. "The 88-Day Story Timeline." *This 'n
That Films,* This 'n That Films, 2015. Web. 20 Apr. 2015.

Fisher, Victor, ed. *Mark Twain in the West: An Exhibition.* University of
California. Berkeley, CA: The Bancroft Library, The Mark Twain Papers and
Project, 2013. Print.

Gillis, William R. *Goldrush Days with Mark Twain.* New York: Albert &
Charles Boni,1930. Print.

---. *Memories of Mark Twain and Steve Gillis, Personal Recollections Of
The Famous Humorist.* Kessinger Publishing, LLC, 2008. Print.

Motlock, Wallace, ed. *Calaveras County Gold Rush Stories.* San Andreas,
CA: Calaveras County Historical Society, 2005. Print.

Paine, Albert Bigelow. *Mark Twain, a Biography.* 3 volumes. New York:
Harper & Bros.,1912. Print.

Twain, Mark. *The Adventures of Huckleberry Finn.*

---. *The Adventures of Tom Sawyer.*

---. *The Autobiography of Mark Twain.* Ed. Charles Neider. New York:
Harper & Row, 1959. Print.

---. *The Five Jumps of the Calaveras Frog.* Angels Camp Museum Exhibit
Booklet. Angels Camp, CA: Angels Camp Museum, 2010. Print.

---. *Life on the Mississippi.*

---. *Roughing It.* Eds. Harriet Elinor Smith and Edgar Marques Branch. The Mark
Twain Project of the Bancroft Library, Berkeley University of California
Press, 1993. Print.

Williams, George III. *Mark Twain: His Adventures in Aurora and Mono
Lake.* Carson City, NV: Tree By The River Publishing Trust, 1987. Print.

---. *Mark Twain: His Life in Virginia City, Nevada.* Carson City, NV: Tree
By The River Publishing Trust, 1985. Print.

---. *Mark Twain and the Jumping Frog of Calaveras County.* Carson City,
NV: Tree By The River Publishing Trust, 1989. Print.

Resources Consulted

Caron, James E. *Mark Twain: Unsanctified Newspaper Reporter.*
University of Missouri Press, 2011. Print.

Clark, William B. *Gold Districts of California, Bulletin 193.* California
Department of Conservation, California Geological Survey, 2005. Print.

De Quille, Dan. *The Big Bonanza: The Story of the Comstock Lode.* New
York: Alfred A. Knopf, 1947. Print.

Limbaugh, Ronald H. and Willard P. Fuller, Jr. *Calaveras Gold: The Impact
of Mining in a Mother Lode County.* University of Nevada Press, 2003. Print.

Mace, O. Henry: *Between the Rivers: A History of Early Calaveras County,
California.* Murphys, CA: Paul Groh Press, 1991. Print.

Mark Twain. Dir: Ken Burns. Florentine Films, 2001. DVD.

Powers, Ron. *Mark Twain: A Life.* New York: Free Press, 2005. Print.

Photos

All of the photos you see in this book have been archived and protected by these
organizations:

The Bank of Stockton Archives
P. O. Box 1110
Stockton, CA 95201

The Calaveras County Historical Society
30 N. Main Street
P. O. Box 721
San Andreas, CA 95249

The Mark Twain Papers & Project
University of California, Berkeley
The Bancroft Library, Room 475
Berkeley, CA 94720 - 6000

The Nevada Historical Society
1650 North Virginia Street
Reno, NV 89503

The Tuolumne County Historical Society
158 Bradford Street
Sonora, CA 95370-4920

Photos and Illustrations

Front Cover Montage – see page 2
Back Cover Author Photo – Randy Lewis, *Los Angeles Times* Staff Writer

The following photos were supplied by the Mark Twain Project and Bancroft Library, University of California, Berkeley. If available, the call numbers are listed.

PH 00058   Jumping Frog Cartoon by Frederick Waddy (1872)   Cover, 136
PH 00002   Sam Clemens at 18 years of age 1
PH 00018   Sam Clemens Bicknell Engraving Cover
PH 02570   Jane Lampton Clemens 13
PH 00001   Sam Clemens Daguerreotype (1850)   17
PH 02573   Henry Clemens 24
PH 02576   Orion Clemens 37

BANC PIC 1905.6302—PIC "C" Street, Virginia City 55
BANC PIC 1905.17500.49:026 Wells Fargo Stagecoach, Virginia City 59

The following photos are available but not yet catalogued by Bancroft Library:
Jackass Hill Cabin with Jim Gillis and Others (courtesy of John Meiser) 67
Jackass Hill, Billy Gillis standing Next to Cabin 68
Jackass Hill, Billy Gillis Seated under an Oak Tree 97

Occidental Hotel 82
Maguire's Academy of Music 85

From the Nevada Historical Society:
Joe Goodman 46
Composing Room of Territorial Enterprise 47
Virginia City (1865) 49

From Calaveras County Historical Society:
The Town of Melones and New Melones Reservoir 3
Robinson's Ferry on the Stanislaus 77
Angels Camp Hotel 79, Cover
Old Miner's Shack 135
Angels Camp Mines 147, 148

From Tuolumne Historical Society:
Swerner's Store, Tuttletown 71

From Bank of Stockton Archives:
Jim Gillis Seated Under an Oak Tree, Cover, 74

Angels Camp Museum:
Replica of Mark Twain Cabin in Parade 145

James Fletcher, Cabin Replica on Jackass Hill 3
Mariusz Blach, Vista of Lake Tahoe Today 39
Susie Hoffman, "On Your Mark" frog photo 144
Connie Strawbridge, Angels Camp Clothesline 145, Author photo 151

Illustrations

The pen and ink drawings in this book were first published in Mark Twain's first editions of Roughing It (1872) and Life on the Mississippi (1883) and are in the public domain.

From Life on the Mississippi:
"Our Permanent Ambition." 19
"Besieging the Pilot." 20
"Learning the River." 22
"I Hit Brown a Good Honest Blow." 26
"Henry and I Sat Chatting." 28
The Explosion. 30
The Hospital Ward. 32
'Let a Leadsman Cry. " 'Half Twain.' " 34

From *Roughing It*:
His Maiden Battle. 36
Our Morning Ride 38
Fire at Lake Tahoe. 41
Worth Nothing. 42
As City Editor. 44
Dreams Dissipated. 61
Slinking. 65
The Old Collegiate. 72
Striking a Pocket. 73

Calaveras County Visitor Resources

Angels Camp Museum
753 South Main St.
Angels Camp, CA 95222
209-736-2963

Calaveras County Arts Council
PO Box 250
22 North Main St.
San Andreas, CA 95249
209-754-1774

Calaveras County Chamber of Commerce
PO Box 1075
39 North Main St.
San Andreas, CA 95249
209-754-5400

Calaveras County Fair and Jumping Frog Jubilee
PO Box 489
101 Frogtown Rd.
Angels Camp, CA 95222
209-736-2561

Calaveras County Historical Society
PO Box 721
30 North Main St.
San Andreas, CA 95249
209-754-1050

Calaveras County Museum Complex
30 North Main St.
San Andreas, CA. 95249
209-754-1058

Calaveras County Visitors Bureau
PO Box 637
1192 South Main St.
Angels Camp, CA 95222
209-736-0049

Camps Restaurant
676 McCauley Ranch Rd.
Angels Camp, CA 95222
209-736-8181

Calaveras Winegrape Alliance
P. O. Box 2492
Murphys, CA 95247
866-806-9463

Greenhorn Creek Resort
711 McCauley Ranch Rd.
Angels Camp, CA 95222
888-736-5900

Manzanita Writers Press
PO Box 632
San Andreas, CA 95249
209-754-0577

Murphys Old Timers Museum
470 Main St.
Murphys, CA 95247
209-728-1160

Tuolumne County Historical Society
158 Bradford St.
Sonora, CA 95370
209-532-1317

Tuolumne County Museum
158 Bradford St.
Sonora, CA 95370
209-532-1317